Screenplay Library

Edited by Matthew J. Bruccoli
Irwin R. Blacker,
Consulting Editor

San Francisco

A Screenplay
By Anita Loos

Edited By Matthew J. Bruccoli
Afterword by Anita Loos

Southern Illinois University Press
Carbondale and Edwardsville
Feffer & Simons, Inc.
London and Amsterdam

Library of Congress cataloguing in Publication Data

Loos, Anita, 1894–
  San Francisco: a screen play.

  (Screenplay library)
  1. San Francisco—Earthquake and fire, 1906—
Drama. I. Bruccoli, Matthew Joseph, 1931–
II. San Francisco. [Motion picture] III. Series.
PN1997.S17119L6 1978   791.43'7   78-9034
ISBN 0-8093-0876-2
ISBN 0-8093-0877-0 pbk.

Preface

By Irwin R. Blacker

This reading version for *San Francisco* is the screenplay as it would have appeared in its final form. The only revisions made in this script are in the format, which now follows that generally used in production today. Over the years several changes have taken place in the format of a script. Among these is the increasing use of the master scene. As any scene will be shot from several different angles and often as many as half a dozen different times, the camera directions are left to the discretion of the director. There are several reasons for multiple coverage, one of which is that it gives the director alternatives in case any one shot does not work out. Another is that the director can recreate the scene in the editing room. The director does not want to be limited in the ways he can envision a scene. For these reasons almost no camera shots are called by the writer any longer, and scenes that take place in one room will usually be broken down by the director and put together again by the director and editor. The scene that takes place in a single interior setting is now known as a master scene.

When *San Francisco* was written, writers were given greater leeway in suggesting how they wanted the picture on the screen. The 1936 script carried direction in detail for both general activity on the part of the actors as well as detailed dialogue direction. Little of this would be found in a script written today. There is a growing independence of function between the writer and the director, in the sense that the writer is responsible for what is on the screen and the director for how it gets there.

One other aspect of *San Francisco* makes it very interesting for the reader: it was an original script. The original script, while not unknown in the days of the major studios and mass feature production, was rare. The western and musical usually were original scripts, but dramatic scripts usually were adapted from stage plays, novels, and short stories. The practice of the studios was to have synopses made for most novels, many short stories, and many non-fiction books. No studio executive could be expected to read all of the books or plays or scripts. The selections were made from the synopses. The practice remains to this day on a much smaller scale.

San Francisco was made at MGM during the years of Louis B. Mayer. He is reputed rarely to have read any script, and it was at MGM that the studio Scheherazade came into being. One morning each week the studio executives would meet and listen to someone who had studied the synopses tell them the stories. If there were a general rejection, the Scheherazade was told to go on to the next story. If Mr. Mayer clutched his fist under his heart and said that it "gets me here," the story was bought and the production scheduled. But the original script, such as San Francisco, had a more difficult time. Without the security of a publisher having bought it or a producer having created it for Broadway, the original story came into the studio on shaky legs. For many years there was an Academy Award for Best Original Story as a thing apart from the script. There were many fine writers who never learned to write anything but a story. Others were brought in to turn the story into a script. In some instances a secretary was given the task of taking the story and typing it into script form.

As the head of his own production unit within the studio structure, Irving Thalberg probably would have presented his story idea for approval himself as a matter of courtesy. The great advantage that San Francisco would have had as an original script was the fact that Thalberg was producing it. The contemporary original script to this day finds its greatest strength in the name of its executive producer. In Thalberg's case, he was assuming the responsibility for seeing that the film came into the film can as presented and that it would not have a cost over-run of more than 10 percent of the estimated budget. These circumstances in no way lessen the quality of any original script, but they help explain how and why some scripts are filmed and others are not.

In reading San Francisco one can see several instances in which the writer informs the reader what the character is thinking. For a reading script this makes sense and may even help the actor and director to understand what the writer had in mind. Today the writer would be told that there is no camera small enough to get inside the actor's head and that the thoughts must be dropped or revealed by the action of the character. Such comments would never be allowed to remain in a script. In preparing *San Francisco* for publication, Anita Loos's revisions have been placed where the revisions would appear in the context of the finished film. Under production conditions, the pages with the revised shots are duplicated on a different color paper with the date of the revision on each revised page so that each person working on the film knows that he is working from the most recent version. It is common practice to remove the old pages from the context of the script. In time there might be as many as ten different colored pages in a script. If another major revision is made after that, the script is usually duplicated in its entirety in still another color. This practice has not changed over the years, and anyone looking at old studio scripts is often faced with a rainbow of color.

The montage of the earthquake of San Francisco has become a classic in American montage. Richard Brooks, the writer-director-producer, made a point of screening *San Francisco* before shooting the fire scenes in *Elmer Gantry*. (He says that the montage did not quite meet his needs, but he did build upon it as a base.) In this script the writer asked for montages as done by Slavko Vorkapich, the MGM specialist who is considered one of the great frame-by-frame aestheticians.

There were twenty-four retakes made in this script, and in one instance there was a retake of a retake. There is clear indication in the script that Miss Loos was working closely with the director and was able to tailor her revisions to the film as it was screened daily. This is a luxury generally not available to either the writer or director now when independent production takes the writer to another project and possibly another studio or remote location after he has finished his script and before it is produced. The script of *San Francisco* reveals the time of the large studio operation, the luxury of major retakes, and the continuing availability of studio-contract actors, directors and writers.

San Francisco
A Screenplay

Credits

Screenplay by Anita Loos based on a story by Robert Hopkins. Musical director, Herbert Stothart. Editor, Tom Held. Photography, Oliver T. Marsh. Art director, Cedric Gibbons. Songs: "San Francisco," by Gus Kahn and Bronislau Kaper; "Would You?" by Arthur Freed and Nacio Herb Brown; "The One Love" by Kahn, Kaper, and Walter Jurmann. Sound recording, Douglas Shearer. Produced by John Emerson and Bernard H. Hyman for MGM. Directed by W. S. Van Dyke. Running time, 115 minutes.

Blackie Norton	Clark Gable
Mary Blake	Jeanette MacDonald
Father Tim Mullin	Spencer Tracy
Jack Burley	Jack Holt
Mrs. Burley	Jessie Ralph
Mat	Ted Healy
Trixie	Shirley Ross
Della Bailey	Margaret Irving
Babe	Harold Huber
Sheriff	Edgar Kennedy
Professor	Al Shean
Signor Baldini	William Ricciardi
Chick	Kenneth Harlan
Alaska	Roger Imhof
Tony	Charles Judels
Red Kelly	Russell Simpson
Freddie Duane	Bert Roach
Hazeltine	Warren B. Hymer

San Francisco

FADE IN:

ARTWORK OF SAN FRANCISCO
Over a beautiful silhouette of old San Francisco . . . before the
fire, the title reads:
> On April 18, 1906, the city of San Francisco met destruc-
> tion. To San Franciscans it was destroyed by fire—
> but fire or earthquake—the old San Francisco—the
> wicked, ribald, licentious San Francisco—ceased to
> exist at—

The title DISSOLVES TO:
> *exactly five-twelve a.m.*
> *April 18—1906.*

The title first starts to shake and then to burn. As it is being
consumed by flames, the title DISSOLVES. As the title dissolves,
there is an o.s. sudden din of HORNS BLOWING, PEOPLE SHOUT-
ING, MUSIC, ETC., ETC. The title DISSOLVES TO:
> San Francisco
> "New Year's Eve—1905."

DISSOLVE TO:

EXT   CITY HALL   NIGHT
City Hall is especially illuminated. A band is stationed on the
stair landing playing RAGTIME. People are dancing in the street.
Excited laughing faces—all types—are glimpsed: a Chinaman
with his little child sitting perched on his shoulder, two young
lovers stopping in the din to kiss, a toothless bum who is calling
out "Happy New Year."

POODLE DOG RESTAURANT
There's a jam of people in the street in front of the Poodle Dog

Restaurant with its flashing sign. Elegant customers are looking
out windows on every floor to hear the midnight din. One girl
crying "Happy New Year" breaks a bottle of champagne on the
window sill.

                                                    DISSOLVE TO:

STREET NEAR LOTTA'S FOUNTAIN
It is filled with revellers. A victoria, driven by a very smart man
in evening dress, comes along. Seated on the horse is an
elegantly-dressed society girl in evening dress but very dishevelled, wearing the man's silk hat. People from the street wave at
her, BLOW HORNS and CALL OUT. A young man runs through
the scene.

                        YOUNG MAN
                        (shouting)
            There's wine in Lotta's fountain, folks. Lotta's foun-
            tain's running *wine*!
Everybody in the street starts off toward Lotta's fountain.

                        PEOPLE (OS)
                (steadily increasing in number)
            Wine in Lotta's fountain! Lotta's fountain's running
            wine! Wine in Lotta's fountain!
The CAMERA FOLLOWS THE CROWD around the corner right up
to Lotta's fountain. On a truck backed up to the fountain is a
sign reading:
            Drink with Freddy Duane
            America's Favorite Wine Agent
Surrounding the fountain is a noisy, jostling crowd. A number
of smart young men in evening dress wearing bartenders'
aprons are opening wine and pouring it into the fountain, while
others are dipping it up in tin cups and serving it to the crowd.
DUANE, a big, fat, hearty man-of-the-world type, in evening
dress, is directing the placing of the last case of champagne from
the truck backed up to the fountain. From the driver's seat of the
truck,

                        TRUCK DRIVER
                        (calling down)
            Shall we bring any more, Mr. Duane?

DUANE
(calling up)
Bring all we've got! Empty the warehouse!

TRUCK DRIVER
You bet!
As the driver starts,

BLACKIE (OS)
I'll take a thousand cases at the same price.
CAMERA PANS TO REVEAL BLACKIE NORTON. He is in evening dress with silk hat, an Inverness overcoat—the cape of which swings back from his shoulders, and he carries a gold-headed cane.

DUANE
(warmly)
Hello, Blackie!

BLACKIE
Hello, Freddy!
Duane proudly looks off at the crowd.

DUANE
Great sight, eh?
Blackie kiddingly pats him on the shoulder.

BLACKIE
Great advertising.

DUANE
(grinning disarmingly)
Sure!
There's a BIG BLARE OF MUSIC and the flaring up of torches. Blackie and Duane look up.

BLACKIE
(calling)
Hello, Della! Happy New Year!
CAMERA PANS to take in a victoria in which is seated a large, handsome woman, DELLA, and several girl cafe entertainers. It is followed by a parade of other victorias similarly laden. The

parade is accompanied by a GERMAN BRASS BAND with a trained bear and a gang of kids. In answer to Blackie's greeting,

                    DELLA
                (very refined)
        The same to you, Mr. Norton.

                   BLACKIE
                  (to girls)
            Happy New Year, girls!

The girls, extremely refined, answer Blackie with restrained and lady like nods.

                    DUANE
            (to Blackie, kiddingly)
        You know everyone, don't you?

                   BLACKIE
                  (grinning)
        Everyone that's worth knowing.

At which point a FIRE ENGINE comes tearing down the street followed by a hook and ladder truck. It has to slow up as it rounds the corner through the crowd.

                MAN IN CROWD
            (calling to fireman)
            Where's the fire?

                   FIREMAN
                (calling back)
            On the Barbary Coast!

                   BLACKIE
                  (alarmed)
        The Coast? Maybe it's my joint!

Pushing people out of the way, Blackie runs and jumps up onto the fire truck.

                                    DISSOLVE TO:

OLD FRAME BUILDING
An old frame building, downstairs a joint and upstairs a rooming house, is in flames. A crowd surrounds it. The fire truck with BLACKIE on board arrives and stops.

> FIREMAN ON TRUCK
> (to Blackie)
> Well—it ain't your place, Mr. Norton.

> BLACKIE

It isn't hot enough for my joint!
At which point—there are o. s. SHRIEKS and VOICES calling "Look out! They're going to jump!" Everyone looks up. TWO CHILDREN stand in the window on the top story. There's a horrified MURMUR from the crowd—then dead SILENCE. The children look down and jump. The children land in a blanket held by firemen and by entertainers in stage makeup. The roof of the building starts to cave in.
Blackie calls to a fireman passing with a hose:

> BLACKIE

Is everyone out of there?

> FIREMAN
> (calling back)
> Okay! They're all out.

As Blackie turns to go,

> BLACKIE

Happy New Year.

> FIREMAN

Same to you.

DISSOLVE TO:

NEAR PACIFIC STREET   BLACKIE
On the way to Pacific Street Blackie passes revellers—sailors, girls—society slummers—Chinese, etc., etc. O.s. a LOUD BLARE OF MUSIC swells up—coming from the joints on Pacific Street.

> A JOINT PROPRIETOR

Hello, Blackie! Happy New Year!

> BLACKIE

Same to you, pal!

> HUSKY-VOICED FEMALE

Happy New Year, Blackie!

BLACKIE

Thanks, sister. Same to you.

Blackie swings around the corner into the Paradise Music Hall.

INT   PARADISE MUSIC HALL

BLACKIE ENTERS and starts toward the check room. In the b.g. we see the gambling room going at full speed. On the stage, TRIXIE, leading the chorus in the New Year's Eve number, is just starting down the runway. As Blackie goes, people he passes greet him right and left: "Hello, Blackie," "Happy New Year, Blackie," etc.

BLACKIE

(in answer)

Hello, sucker! Same to you! (etc.)

The hat check boy hops to take Blackie's hat and coat.

HAT CHECK BOY

Happy New Year, Mr. Norton!

BLACKIE

Thanks!

Blackie looks at the hat check boy.

BLACKIE (cont'd)

How's that mother of yours this evening?

HAT CHECK BOY

She's a lot better!

Blackie pats his shoulder.

BLACKIE

That's the stuff!

At which point BABE, the bouncer of the Paradise, steps up.

BABE

Where's the fire, Boss?

BLACKIE

Dupont Street. The old Bristol.

By which time Trixie has jumped down off the runway and appears at Blackie's side. During the remainder of the scene in b.g. the chorus comes down the runway and into the audience removing their outer skirts on which are painted *1905* to reveal *1906* on tights underneath. Trixie approaches Blackie, obviously in love with him.

>   TRIXIE
>   Happy New Year, Blackie.

>   BLACKIE
>   Happy New Year, honey.

Blackie pinches her cheek. Trixie gazes right into Blackie's face.

>   TRIXIE
>   (from her heart)
>   Gee—*I want it to be happy!*

Blackie LAUGHS.

>   BABE
>   (to Trixie)
>   The fire was at the Bristol.

>   TRIXIE
>   Oh—that trap.

Trixie looks down at Blackie's shoes.

>   TRIXIE (cont'd)
>   Why your shoes are all muddy!

Grabbing a napkin from a table, Trixie shoves up a chair for Blackie to put his foot on and proceeds to clean his shoes.

>   BABE
>   (preoccupied about fire)
>   Gee Blackie—this makes the third fire we've had in a week!

>   BLACKIE
>   (kidding, but none the less concerned)
>   Yeah. We'd all better buy asbestos suits.

>   BABE
>   *I'll say so!*

Looking down at Trixie, Blackie notes a flashy dog collar she's wearing.

BLACKIE
Thought I told you not to wear that thing!
Trixie looks up from cleaning his shoes.

TRIXIE
(pleadingly)
Oh, honey—I think it's nice.
Blackie rips it off.

BLACKIE
I think it makes you look cheap!
Blackie hands it to her. Trixie feels her throat where the collar tore the skin and, tears in her eyes, continues to clean Blackie's shoes. Babe starts to go, then remembering something, stops.

BABE
(aside, so Trixie won't hear)
Oh, Blackie—Mrs. Forrestall's over there—with a party of swells.
(with a wink)
She's been asking for you.

BLACKIE
(amused and interested)
That so?
Saying which, Blackie leaves Trixie in the midst of her humble service and heads for Mrs. Forrestall's table. As he goes, people greet him from every table.

CUSTOMERS
Hello, Blackie! How are you, Blackie! etc. etc.

BLACKIE
(greeting them)
Hello, Pal! How are you, chumps?
Blackie comes up to a table where a very pretty society woman, EUNICE FORRESTALL, sits with a party of smart types—all very tight.

BLACKIE
(to Mrs. Forrestall)
Hello, Eunice. Happy New Year.

                         MRS. FORRESTALL
     Happy New Year, Blackie.
Mrs. Forrestall reaches up her face to be kissed and Blackie gives
her a big, long kiss. The kiss over, as if remembering something,
Mrs. Forrestall indicates a man at the table.

                         MRS. FORRESTALL
     Oh! I want you to meet my husband.
Everybody LAUGHS.

                         BLACKIE
                    (heartily)
     How d'you do? Happy New Year.

                         FORRESTALL
                    (heartily)
     Happy New Year to you!
O.s. Mat's stage number is introduced. A waiter comes up to
Blackie with wine.

                         BLACKIE
                    (to waiter)
     Mark this on the house.

                         MEMBERS OF FORRESTALL PARTY
     Thanks. Thank you. etc.
Blackie salutes them and starts away, looking o.s. toward the
stage.

                                              CUT TO:

THE STAGE   MAT   BLACKIE'S POV
On stage MAT starts to SING at the top of his lungs. He only
sings a few notes when a wad of serpentine paper soaked in
beer sails through the air almost hitting him in the face. Mat is
outraged but goes right on singing.

THE AUDIENCE   BLACKIE
Annoyed, Blackie looks toward Babe and gives him the office.
Babe gets Blackie's signal and heads into action. A DRUNK is
seated at a table with one of the girls of the Paradise. The Drunk
is soaking another handful of serpentine paper in his glass of

beer, to the protestations of the girl. Babe comes over. The
Drunk looks up, sees Babe towering over him and hesitates.

BABE
(to Drunk, over-polite)

Come on, pal.
Babe grabs the drunk by the coat collar and starts to drag him
out toward the door.

DRUNK

I don't like his singing.
As Babe hustles him along,

BABE
(still sarcastically polite)

But you mustn't hurt the artist's feelings.

DRUNK

His feelings. Well—who is he against so many?
By this time we have heard enough of the song to realize that it
is a tribute to San Francisco. Babe suddenly gets an idea.

BABE

Say—where are you from?

DRUNK
(proudly)

Los Angeles!

BABE

I thought so.
Saying which, Babe looks surreptitiously around to be sure he's
unobserved. Then, still holding the Drunk with one hand, he
gives him a short, quick sock on the button with the other hand
and knocks him cold, proceeding to carry him out. At the
entrance to the Paradise, as Babe hands the Drunk over to a
couple of waiters, with just a nod of his head by way of instruc-
tion, MARY COMES IN, carrying her valise. She is young, very
pretty, and of evident refinement, although at the moment she
appears dazed and somewhat dishevelled. Mary comes up to
Babe and faces him, appearing helpless and exhausted.

MARY
(nervously)
I beg your pardon—are you the manager here?
Babe looks her over.

BABE
Well—I kind of run the joint. What d'you want, sister?

MARY
I'm looking for work.

BABE
Oh.
Babe looks quizzically at her valise.

BABE (cont'd)
Just get to town?

MARY
No. The place where I was living just burned down.
Babe is still looking her over.

BABE
Oh yeah—that trap on Dupont Street. That's tough.
Mary grows increasingly nervous under Babe's boldly admiring
gaze.

MARY
I've . . . I've been looking for work uptown—but there
didn't seem to be any. So I came down here to the Barbary Coast. I've tried at several of the places but—
(she falters)
And she smiles and pathetically shrugs her shoulders to indicate
her lack of luck.

BABE
(warmly—sympathetically but on-the-make)
Well come on and have a little drink.
Saying which, he familiarly takes hold of her arm. Frightened,
Mary pulls away.

MARY
Thank you but—
She looks at him with disarming appeal.

MARY (cont'd)
Couldn't I please see the proprietor?
Babe is affected by her look.

BABE
(heartily)
All right, sister! Come on!
He leads her toward Blackie's box. As they go, Mary, anxious to
return Babe's kindness, tries to make conversation.

MARY
This is the Paradise, isn't it?

BABE
I'll say it is. The hottest spot on the Barbary Coast.
A drunk passes Mary.

A DRUNK
Oh you chicken!
Babe steers Mary protectingly past the drunk.

BABE
(to Drunk)
Watch yourself, brother.
By which time they are near Blackie's box.

BABE
(to Mary, kindly)
Just a minute, honey.
And Babe heads o.s. for Blackie.

THE STAGE   MAT
Mat, singing at the top of his lungs, comes to the finish of it. He
and the girls make an exit to enthusiastic APPLAUSE.

BLACKIE'S BOX   BLACKIE
Blackie is seated lounging back in his chair, looking off over the
APPLAUSE reaction of the crowd when BABE ENTERS.

BABE
There's a little lady out here looking for a job. She was
burned out in that fire at the Bristol.

BLACKIE
(a little indifferently)
Yeah?

BABE
She's not bad.

BLACKIE
All right. Bring her in.
As BABE GOES OUT of the box,

SOMEONE (OS)
Everybody waltz!
O.s. the orchestra starts up a WALTZ. BABE REENTERS, ushering
MARY IN.

BABE
This is Mr. Norton. He owns the joint.

MARY
How do you do?
BABE GOES OUT. Blackie leans back, making himself comfort-
able as he looks Mary over.

BLACKIE
Well, sister, what's your racket?

MARY
(uncomfortable, nervous)
I'm . . . I'm a singer.

BLACKIE
(matter-of-fact)
Let's see your legs.

MARY
(defensively)
I said I'm a singer.

BLACKIE
All right. Let's see your legs.
Pulling herself together, Mary raises her skirts a few inches. Tol-
erant of what to him is a pose,

BLACKIE
(kindly)
Well come on! Let's see 'em!

Blackie gestures for Mary to raise her skirt higher. Mary hesitates a brief moment—then—choking back her distaste—raises her skirts a little higher. Blackie looks with interest at her legs.

BLACKIE
Hmm. A little thin for down here.

He gestures off toward the MUSIC.

BLACKIE
D'you know that number?

MARY
(hesitant)
Yes.

BLACKIE
Let's hear you sing it.

Mary hesitates a brief second—then—still standing right before Blackie starts to SING. Blackie sits back, utterly unmoved by her singing, coolly taking her in. Once in awhile, people going by the box glance up at her, but nobody pays any great attention. Bravely Mary struggles through the ordeal, near the end of which MAT APPEARS in the back of the box and listens, none too impressed. At the END OF THE SONG, Mary looks anxiously at Blackie for his decision.

BLACKIE
(casually)
You've got a pretty fair set of pipes, kid. What would you say to seventy-five a week?

Mary looks at him for a long moment—just looks—and then suddenly crumpling, falls in a faint at his feet. Blackie remains seated.

BLACKIE
I guess she fainted!

Mat's disgusted with Mary.

                              MAT
                         (to Blackie)
          Give me seventy-five bucks a week and I'd drop dead!
                                              FADE OUT:

FADE IN:

EXT   FRONT OF PARADISE
BLACKIE comes out of the Paradise and goes up steps at the side
leading to his apartment.
                                              DISSOLVE TO:

INT   PARLOR   BLACKIE'S APARTMENT   MARY
Mary is seated at a small table just finishing supper in the sitting
room of Blackie's apartment over the Paradise. JOW LEE, a
Chinese servant, is in attendance. The room is floridly furnished
in rococo luxury. A fancy gold clock on the mantlepiece registers
three-thirty. The MUSIC from downstairs suddenly gets LOUD-
ER as the door opens. Mary looks up. BLACKIE ENTERS, then
closes the door DIMMING THE MUSIC.

                            BLACKIE
              Well, kiddo! Did you have some rest?
Though fortified by food, Mary is yet ill at ease.

                             MARY
              Yes, thanks.

                            BLACKIE
              Good!
                         (to Jow Lee)
              Get rid of this, will you?
Jow Lee gives an approving glance at Mary.

                            JOW LEE
              Yes, sir.
Jow Lee proceeds to remove tray.

                             MARY
                      (preoccupied, worried)
              I want to thank you, Mr. Norton, for your
              kindness and—
As Blackie looks her over, he gestures and:

BLACKIE
Aw—never mind the etiquette.

MARY
But it was stupid of me—fainting like that. I haven't eaten much today and—
Mary looks up with an anxious smile.

MARY (cont'd)
It's true, isn't it? You *did* offer me a job?

BLACKIE
(amused at her, quizzical)
What's the matter? Want it in writing?
Mary is confused—worried—fearful that she has made a faux pas.

MARY
Oh, no.
Blackie looks her over and sees her confusion. Then, trying to put her at her ease,

BLACKIE
(agreeably)
You're all right, honey. What's your name?
Mary looks at him.

MARY
Mary Blake.
Trying to make her feel at home,

BLACKIE
(with exaggerated interest)
Mary Blake, eh? That's catchy!
Mary looks at Blackie.

BLACKIE (cont'd)
Just make yourself at home, babe. I'll be right with you.
Saying which, BLACKIE GOES OFF into the bedroom. Looking after him askance, Mary begins to be worried.

BLACKIE'S BEDROOM   BLACKIE
Blackie's in his bedroom, calling through to the other room. His

manner is that of an important person trying to put an unimportant one at ease.

                    BLACKIE
          (kindly)
     Where'd you hail from?

                    MARY (OS)
     Colorado. Benson, Colorado. That's near Denver.

                    BLACKIE
     I see.
Blackie starts to take off his coat and vest.

                    BLACKIE (cont'd)
     Been here long?

                    MARY (OS)
          (still worried)
     No—only a few weeks.

                    BLACKIE
     Where've you been working?

                    MARY (OS)
     In the Benson Public Library.

                    BLACKIE
          (a little surprised)
     Singing?

                    MARY (OS)
     Oh, no. I sang in church Sundays.
Blackie's at his dresser, taking off his watch—wondering a little
if she's telling the truth.

                    BLACKIE
     So you sang in the *church choir*?
Blackie takes out some money.

                    MARY (OS)
          (sensing his disbelief)
     Well—it was my father's old church and—
Blackie begins to think she may be lying.

                         BLACKIE
And your father's a *preacher*?
Saying which, he picks up his watch and money, opens the
dresser drawer, puts them in it, closes it and locks it, putting the
key under the dresser scarf. Meanwhile, Mary pauses before re-
plying.

                         MARY (OS)
            He was.

                         BLACKIE
                    (chuckling)
            I see. He got onto himself?
In resentment at Blackie's cynicism,

                         MARY (OS)
                    (bursts out)
            He died four years ago!

                         BLACKIE
                    (amused—incredulous)
            Oh—I get you.
BLACKIE GOES OFF, back into the parlor/sitting room.

PARLOR   MARY
BLACKIE ENTERS the parlor where Mary still sits.

                         BLACKIE
            The orphan child of a country parson!

                         MARY
            After all, Mr. Norton, there *are* such men as country
            parsons and sometimes they do have daughters!
Blackie admires her for her spirit.

                         BLACKIE
            Well—that sort of puts me in my place, don't it?
                    (with interest)
            Who brought you to Frisco?

                         MARY
            Nobody. My mother helped me get here.
Blackie moves close to her.

BLACKIE

I see.
Mary begins to be afraid.

MARY

You don't believe me, do you?

BLACKIE
(very genially, chuckling)
Why, sure I believe you. You're all right, Mary!
Blackie puts one hand on her shoulder. Mary looks up at him
frightened—dazed—unable to make a move.

BLACKIE (cont'd)

Tomorrow we're going to get rid of those Benson glad
rags and dig you up some swell new scenery.
Blackie fingers her hair.

BLACKIE (cont'd)

You've got all the makings, kid! Why, you're going to
do great!
Saying which, Blackie puts his arm about Mary and starts to
draw her to him. Mary, now panicky, pulls away.

BLACKIE (cont'd)

What's the matter?
At last coming to a full realization of what he expects of her,
Mary pulls herself together and with a sudden movement,
turns, hurries to where her valise lies on the floor, picks it up,
and heads for the door.

BLACKIE
(surprised)
Where you going?

MARY
(frightened)
I don't know.
Blackie blocks her way.

BLACKIE
(kindly, tolerantly)

Wait a minute! You don't have to stall me, honey.
>   (chuckles)
I *wrote* that old spiel you just pulled—parson father—
sacrificing mother—the whole thing—years ago! I
guess you've got some John on the string, haven't you?

                    MARY
              (still frightened)
Please let me go.

                    BLACKIE
I see.
He looks at her a moment longer, then:

              BLACKIE (cont'd)
What's the railroad fare here from Benson?
Mystified, Mary looks up at him.

                    MARY
Why—why, I paid sixteen eighty.
Blackie reaches in his pocket.

                    BLACKIE
              (chuckling)
If there's anything I admire it's a woman you can trust
out of town.
Blackie SLAMS two ten-dollar gold pieces down on the table.

              BLACKIE (cont'd)
Send for the mug you're stuck on.
Mary looks at him—just looks. He turns, goes to the bedroom
door, then turns again.

              BLACKIE (cont'd)
It's pretty late. You can bunk here if you want to.
BLACKIE ENTERS the bedroom, closes the door. Mary looks after
him for a moment, then starts packing her things hurriedly. She
HEARS the DOOR OPEN, turns, startled. At the door BLACKIE
inserts a key in her side of the door, and gives her a quizzical
look, then GOES BACK INTO the bedroom closing the door after
him. Mary thinks a moment, then crosses tentatively to the door
and locks it.

BLACKIE'S BEDROOM   BLACKIE
Blackie smiles quizzically as he HEARS the LOCK CLICK. He's
been a sucker, all right. He shrugs his shoulders and starts OUT
OF SCENE to get undressed.

LIVING ROOM   MARY
Mary wonders what she should do—decides it's late and she'll
stay. She tries to go to sleep on a small sofa, which is too short
and too narrow. Her efforts on the sofa are somewhat comical.
Finally, she picks up a couple of cushions and starts for the
floor.

BLACKIE'S BEDROOM   BLACKIE
Blackie's reflection is seen in the mirror of his dresser as he approaches to put out the light. He is in pajamas. He pulls a "low
chain," dimming the light, and turns away, pauses, turns back,
pulls "high chain," brightening the light. He looks at himself in
the mirror, smiles and salutes.

                    BLACKIE
          Good night, sucker.

He pulls the "low chain," dimming the light, and EXITS the
SCENE.

LIVING ROOM   MARY
Mary tries to make herself comfortable on the floor with the two
cushions. She wriggles around a moment. One cushion cuts her
cheek. She rises slightly and looks down at it. With a smile of
despair, she throws it aside.

INSERT SHOT   CUSHION
On the floor, chair or what-have-you, as the cushion lands, re-
vealing for the first time its embroidered inscription:
WELCOME TO SAN FRANCISCO

FADE OUT.

FADE IN:

INT   CLOSE SHOT   GYMNASIUM   BLACKIE   DAY
Blackie's boxing with a tall handsome young man, TIM MULLIN.
CAMERA PULLING BACK REVEALS gymnasium. In the b.g. can
be seen members of the gymnasium (all Pacific Street types)
exercising, swinging clubs, etc., etc. MAT comes up to the ring,
watches them box a moment, then:

MAT
(to Blackie, rather casually)
Say, Boss—the Professor's over at the joint waiting to
rehearse that new girl and she's never showed up.

BLACKIE
(casually)
That so?

MAT
Guess we can forget her, can't we?

BLACKIE
Yeah—forget her.
Mat WHISTLES in relief and wipes his brow.

MAT
Am I relieved!

TIM

(to Mat)

No good, eh?

Blackie LAUGHS sarcastically.

BLACKIE

I'll say she's good. Why—her father was a *preacher*!

MAT

A preacher? Gee—that's an old one!

Mat lets out a BIG GUFFAW.

TIM

Well—maybe her father was a preacher!

Blackie LAUGHS, then indicating Tim:

BLACKIE

(to Mat)

He still believes in Santy Claus.

TIM

(to Blackie)

The trouble with you is you don't believe in anything!

BLACKIE

That's where I'm smart!

And Blackie lands a pretty good sock. Tim rallies, then:

TIM

Did you say smart?

BLACKIE

That's what I said.

Tim lands a sock which sends Blackie to the floor in a sitting position. Mat and Tim LAUGH. Blackie remains on the floor, laboriously getting his breath as:

BLACKIE

I'm a sucker if I ever learn anything! For twenty years this big mug has mauled me around and made a chump out of me and I always come back for more!

> MAT
> (laughing)
> Aw—he got to bed earlier'n you did.

> TIM
> (to Blackie, amused)
> Come on—get up!

> BLACKIE
> (exaggeratedly, to Tim, grinning)
> I'm not going to move *from this spot* until you're *out* of the building!

> TIM
> (laughing)
> All right, kid.

Tim gives Blackie an affectionate pat on the shoulder.

> TIM (cont'd)
> See you later.

Tim gets over the rope and GOES OFF toward the dressing rooms. Mat looks after Tim.

> MAT
> That guy sure packs a wallop!

Blackie peers around cautiously.

> BLACKIE
> (quizzically)
> Has he gone?

> MAT
> (laughing)
> Yeah.

Blackie laboriously starts to get up when Mat looks off.

> MAT (cont'd)
> (surprised)
> Say—*pipe the parade*!

Blackie settles back onto the floor and looks around to see approaching the ring a delegation of joint proprietors—ALASKA—CHICK—RED KELLY and GUS. They are all big shots of the

Coast, dressed in their best—very self-conscious and full of importance. Blackie looks them over as they come up. Alaska is middle-aged, rugged, sweating with importance. Red Kelly is a wiry, hard-headed type, a trace sour. Chick is young, very tough, but trying to appear a solid citizen. Gus is a garrulous German.

> BLACKIE
> Hello, boys—what's the idea—paying New Year's calls?

> ALASKA
> (simultaneously)
> Hello, Blackie. Hello, Mat.

> RED KELLY
> (simultaneously)
> Hello, boys.

> CHICK
> (simultaneously)
> Good morning, Blackie.
> (to Mat)
> Hello.

> GUS
> (simultaneously, to Blackie)
> How's the kid?
> (to Mat)
> Hello, Mat.

Mat salutes in answer. The delegation stops—they all look at Alaska who, as oldest, is spokesmaster. Alaska CLEARS HIS THROAT, then politely gesturing toward a chair at ringside:

> ALASKA
> Blackie, would you like to—

Blackie rubs his hip and:

> BLACKIE
> (quizzically)
> Thanks—someone just showed me to a seat.

Alaska grins, then self-consciously CLEARS HIS THROAT again
and:

ALASKA
(with great importance)
Blackie—we've looked you up to complain about that
fire last night in Dupont Street.

BLACKIE
(kidding)
Complain? Why, I thought it was perfect. Say, what do
you boys *want* in the way of a fire?

Chick pulls up a chair and:

CHICK
(to Alaska, sotto voce)
You talked better at the meetin'—sittin' down!

Chick jerks Alaska roughly into the chair. Red Kelly steps forward.

RED KELLY
Listen, Blackie—Jim Sullivan's kids got trapped in that
fire last night—they had to jump for it!

BLACKIE
I saw them.
(in approbation)
Why, they pulled it off like old-time circus performers!

GUS
(cutting in)
Mr. Norton—you ain't got no kids. But look at me! I got
plenty kids and maybe when I get home I got another
one or two.

CHICK
(to Gus, laughing)
Well, don't go home!

Blackie starts painfully to rise.

BLACKIE
Look boys—put me down for a hundred dollars for Jim
and his kids and tell 'em to—

ALASKA
(cutting in)
That isn't what we came for, Blackie.
Alaska rises.

ALASKA (cont'd)
(importantly)
We want you to let us run you for City Supervisor!
Mat pricks up his ears. Blackie sinks once more into a sitting
position.

BLACKIE
WHAT?

RED KELLY
That's right, Blackie. The only way to get some decent
fire regulations on the Coast is to force 'em through the
City Council.

CHICK
Make 'em tear these here traps down and put up some
brick buildin's!

ALASKA
And you're the only man on the Coast with the—the—
(stumbles for word)

RED KELLY
(cueing him)
Authority!
Alaska points a finger at Blackie and:

ALASKA
(finishes sentence)
—to do it.
Blackie tries to cover the fact that he is greatly pleased.

BLACKIE
Well now, look, boys—you know who's the biggest
landlord on the Coast. It's Jack Burley. I've talked to
him and he's made of granite!

RED KELLY
But we've never put up a real fight before!

ALASKA
And we've never had a *real leader*!

GUS
Und there ain't nobody else what's crazy enough to
fight Jack Burley.

CHICK AND RED KELLY
(to Gus, in unison)
Ix-nay! Shut up!

BLACKIE
(to Gus, quizzically)
Maybe *I'm* not either!

TIM (OS)
I think it's a great idea!
They look up. TIM IS REVEALED standing near the group garbed
in the robes of a Catholic Priest.

TIM
(to the committee, in greeting)
Good morning, boys.

MAT
(enthused)
A "great idea?" Why, it's dynamite! *Supervisor Norton*.
It'd get the joint a million dollars' publicity.
Alaska turns to Blackie.

ALASKA
What do you say?

BLACKIE
Where's the dough going to come from?

CHICK
We'll back you, Blackie!

ALASKA
That's right! Up to the limit!

GUS
(to Tim)
Father Mullin—you speak to him.

TIM
You like a fight, Blackie. Go on!

BLACKIE
Have you all gone nuts?
But Blackie grins.

TIM
(to the men)
I can't do anything with him—I've tried for twenty years.
Tim glances at the clock.

TIM (cont'd)
But maybe *you* can, boys. So long and good luck!

ALL
Good-bye, Father.

BLACKIE
So long, Tim.
Blackie starts to get up as TIM EXITS.

ALASKA
(to Blackie)
Well, Blackie. How about it?
Blackie picks up his bathrobe.

BLACKIE
(evasively)
Come on over and have a drink!
Blackie leads them off toward a side exit, the CAMERA FOLLOW-
ING THEM, Blackie putting on his bathrobe as he goes.

CHICK
Can you see what that big, chesty Nob Hill dude is
gonna say when he hears he's got Blackie to deal with?

BLACKIE
(quizzically cautious)

Yeah! That's just what I'm thinking of!
At which point THEY EXIT into the alley.

EXT   ALLEY   BLACKIE   OTHERS
They reach the alley between the gymnasium and the Paradise.
Blackie looks up and sees MARY standing in the stage doorway.
He hesitates just a brief second, then goes right on as if he
hadn't seen her. Mary, looking on, hears their discussion.

> GUS
> Mr. Norton, I tell you what! You run for City Super-
> visor and the next boy my Lena gives me, I name him
> Blackie after you!

THEY LAUGH.

> RED KELLY
> Aw—name the next half dozen after him!

Blackie LAUGHS—then—passing Mary, swells up a trace—not
unconscious that she's hearing of his aggrandizement.

> BLACKIE
> I think you fellows have all blown your toppers!

> MARY
> (calls after Blackie)
> Oh, Mr. Norton.

Blackie stops.

> BLACKIE
> (casually)
> Yes.

Mat also stops to see what's going to happen—the others
GOING OFF toward the bar.

> MARY
> May I have that job?

> BLACKIE
> Didn't I say so?

> MARY
> Yes . . .

BLACKIE

Well, how many times do you want me to say it?
Saying which, he turns and goes on. Mat looks back at Mary in
utter disgust—then takes his hat, throws it on the floor, and
follows Blackie on to bar.

INT PARADISE BAR BLACKIE MAT OTHERS
The Committee is lined up at the bar giving their orders. The
ordering and serving action is all very fast.

ALASKA
(to bartender)
Make mine Scotch.

BARTENDER

Yes, sir.
The bartender pushes forward a bottle and glass. Alaska starts
to pour his drink. Bartender turns to Red Kelly.

RED KELLY

Scotch.
The bartender gives him a glass.

CHICK
(to bartender)
That's good.

GUS

Me too.
O.s. Mary starts to SING "San Francisco" accompanied by the
Professor, Mary naturally failing to give the song its low-down
Frisco rhythm. Mat stands preoccupied looking back at Mary
o.s.

BLACKIE
(to Mat)
What d'you want, Mat?

MAT
(disgusted)
Chloroform.
Blackie LAUGHS. Then,

                    BLACKIE
                 (to bartender)
        A little water for me.

                    BARTENDER
          Yes, sir.
The bartender proceeds to get him mineral water. Alaska holds
up his drink.

                    ALASKA
        Well—here's to you, Blackie.

                    ALL
                 (in unison)
        Here's to you kiddo. Here's how!
They drink.

                    BLACKIE
                 (simultaneously)
          Thanks.
One by one they all look off toward Mary and begin to take stock
of her beauty.

                    ALASKA
                 (thoughtfully)
        Blackie—ain't she singin' a little slow?

                    BLACKIE
                 (disgustedly)
          Yeah.
Blackie puts down his drink.

                    ALASKA
                 (with pretended disapproval)
        Hope you ain't gone and signed her up.
Blackie notes Alaska feasting his eyes on Mary.

                    BLACKIE
        Why? So you can grab her off for your joint?
They all LAUGH, Alaska guiltily. Blackie slaps Alaska on the
arm, and heads toward Mary, the CAMERA MOVING WITH
HIM. MARY is still SINGING when:

BLACKIE
(roughly cutting in)
Wait a minute!
Mary and the Professor stop.

BLACKIE (cont'd)
(to Mary)
What do you think I'm running—a funeral parlor?
Mary, distressed, says nothing.

PROFESSOR
(coming to her defense)
But Blackie—with a voice like hers it ain't so easy to—

BLACKIE
(cutting in)
Get up!
The Professor, who's been accompanying Mary on the piano,
rises from his seat there. Without sitting down, Blackie starts to
PLAY THE PIANO, tearing off the song in hot rhythm.

BLACKIE (cont'd)
Go on—get started!
Mary hesitates a moment—then SINGS, trying to get into the
rhythm of the Coast. The Professor watches her with sympathy.
Blackie lets her sing a little ways—then as he continues to
play—

BLACKIE
(disgustedly cuts in)
That's not it! Put something into it! *Heat it up!*
Blackie emphasizes the rhythm with his shoulders.

BLACKIE (cont'd)
That's what it's *about*! *San Francisco!* Give it *that*!
Mary BREAKS OFF HER SINGING.

MARY
I can't sing like that!

BLACKIE
(brutally)

Well, that's the way you're *going* to sing it—or you don't sing it for me!
Saying which, he heads OFF away from the piano. The Professor, patting Mary's hand in sympathy, resumes his seat at the piano.

THE BAR   BLACKIE   MAT   OTHERS
As Blackie barges back to his pals,

> BLACKIE
> Oh, Mat.

Mat looks up.

> BLACKIE (cont'd)
> Go get Babe to dig up a contract.

O.s. we hear the Professor and Mary beginning the song, Mary striving to do it as Blackie wishes.

> MAT
> (disgusted)
> A *contract*?

> BLACKIE
> Yeah.

Then Blackie grins at Alaska and:

> BLACKIE (cont'd)
> Guess I better sign that girl up before I change my mind.

As Mat starts to leave,

> MAT
> (disgusted)
> Change your mind? You've *lost* it!

THEY LAUGH.

CLOSE SHOT   MARY
Mary SINGING.

DISSOLVE TO:

CLOSE SHOT   STAGE OF PARADISE   MARY   NIGHT
Mary, dressed in a gaudy stage costume, is SINGING the song as

Blackie commanded. CAMERA PULLING BACK REVEALS the Paradise full of smoke and rowdy customers.

BLACKIE'S BOX   BLACKIE
Blackie sits leaning back in his chair, smoking a cigar and taking Mary all in.

CLOSE SHOT   MARY   BLACKIE'S POV
Mary is seen in profile in her revealing and low cut gown.

CLOSE SHOT   BLACKIE
He studies her closely, obviously pleased and intrigued.

AISLE ACROSS FROM BLACKIE'S BOX   BURLEY   BALDINI
JACK BURLEY, a smartly dressed man of about forty-two, is being shown down the aisle with great deference by the head waiter, followed by BALDINI, an Italian of great distinction and charm (about fifty). BABE hops forward and joins them.

> BABE
> (a little bit overdeferent)
> Good evening, Mr. Burley!

> BURLEY
> Good evening.

Babe gestures toward the box across from Blackie's.

> BABE
> (to head waiter)
> Show Mr. Burley and Signor Baldini to a box.

> HEAD WAITER
> Sure thing. I was going to.

> BURLEY
> (to Babe)
> Is Blackie Norton around?

> BABE
> (with just a flicker of quizzical interest)
> Yes.

> BURLEY
> (a trace imperious)

Tell him I want to see him.

> BABE
> (still quizzical)
You bet.
BABE GOES OFF.

STAGE MARY
Mary finishes her number and goes OFF. The audience AP-
PLAUDS. The PROFESSOR is looking intently off at Baldini. He
turns, glances quickly off toward where Mary is—then, getting a
sudden idea, he heads back stage. MARY comes out in answer to
APPLAUSE and takes a bow, on her face a fixed smile, revealing
her distaste at what she is having to go through.

> PEOPLE IN AUDIENCE (OS)
> You're all right, sweetheart! What're you doing after
> the show?
MARY BOWS HER WAY OFF.

BACK STAGE MARY
Mary comes from the stage. At which point MAT barges into the
scene, ready for his number.

> MAT
> (to Mary)
> Get out of the way!
Mat starts to crowd past her at which point the PROFESSOR AP-
PEARS, and grabs Mat by the coat-tail—holding him back.

> PROFESSOR
> (to Mary with suppressed excitement)
> Go out there and sing *"Ein Hertz das Ist Frei."*
Mat turns to the Professor.

> MAT
> *Who—me?*
Still holding Mat back,

> PROFESSOR
> (to Mary)
> Like you did for me this afternoon!
Mary is surprised.

MAT
(to Professor)
Get back in that orchestra and start my number!
The Professor disregards Mat.

PROFESSOR
(to Mary)
Baldini's out there—of the Tivoli Opera House.
Mary catches her breath.

MARY

Baldini?

MAT
(to the Professor, outraged)
The show's dyin' on its feet!
The Professor pays no attention to Mat—but still hangs onto
him.

PROFESSOR
(to Mary, urgently)
It's your big chance! You've got to take it!

MAT
WHAT'S GOING ON HERE?
Mary pays no attention to Mat.

MARY
But what will Mr. Norton say?
As the Professor starts away,

PROFESSOR
We can't help that!
The PROFESSOR DUCKS OUT, going to the stairs leading into the
orchestra pit, THE CAMERA FOLLOWING HIM a little way, then:

BLACKIE'S BOX   BLACKIE
Blackie is seated, leaning back comfortably, listening in satisfac-
tion to the APPLAUSE following Mary's number. BABE ushers in
BURLEY and BALDINI. Seeing them, BLACKIE jumps up.

BLACKIE
(overly gracious)

Good evening, Burley.
Burley covers his antagonism by being overly friendly.

                    BURLEY
          How are you, Norton?
Burley turns and indicates Baldini.

                    BURLEY (cont'd)
          I'd like to introduce Signor Baldini of the Tivoli Opera
          House.

                    BLACKIE
                 (graciously)
          How do you do, sir?
They shake hands. Blackie gestures them to seats.

                    BLACKIE (cont'd)
          What'll you gentlemen have to drink?
Burley smiles.

                    BURLEY
                 (full of charm)
          Nothing—thanks.
At which point the PROFESSOR barges excitedly up to the rail of
the box, almost overcome by his excitement.

                    PROFESSOR
                 (to Baldini)
          Maestro!
Baldini looks at him, obviously not recognizing him.

                    PROFESSOR (cont'd)
          My name is Hertzen. I played under your direction one
          night in Dresden.

                    BALDINI
                 (warmly)
          Really? I haven't been in Dresden in twenty years.

                    PROFESSOR
          That was the night!
The others react, amused. Covering his amusement, Baldini
shakes his hand.

                    BALDINI
                 (warmly)
I'm happy to see you again.

                   PROFESSOR
Ach! I'm nothing! But, Maestro, we have down here a
voice! A voice that would delight your soul, Maestro! A
voice that—

                    BLACKIE
           (cutting in, amused, tolerantly)
How about going on with the show, Professor?

                   PROFESSOR
               (to Blackie)
Yes, sir. I'm sorry.
The Professor then turns back to Baldini.

               PROFESSOR (cont'd)
This voice, Maestro! If you could hear it in something
really good—if you could hear it as I have heard it in—

                    BLACKIE
             (cutting in, a touch sarcastic)
We're trying to give a show tonight, Professor.

                   PROFESSOR
I'm sorry, Mr. Norton.
The Professor starts to go, then turning to Baldini:

               PROFESSOR (cont'd)
Maestro! If you could only hear—
                 (breaks off)
And we see that an idea is entering his mind.

                    BLACKIE
               (a little annoyed)
Well, how about it?
The Professor's face is alight with an idea.

                   PROFESSOR
               (to Blackie)
    I'm going!

The PROFESSOR LEAVES. Blackie turns, passing his cigarette case to Burley. Baldini is already smoking.

> BLACKIE

Cigarette?

> BURLEY

No, thanks.
> (charmingly casual)
I think you know what I came down here for.

Blackie, engaged in lighting a cigarette, looks up inquiringly.

> BURLEY (cont'd)

I heard this afternoon that you're going to run for the City Council.

> BLACKIE

That's right.

> BURLEY
> (warmly, as if giving friendly advice)
I wouldn't do that if I were you, Norton.

> BLACKIE
> (casually)
Why not?

Burley smiles to cover his real feeling.

> BURLEY

I don't believe you'd like it.

> BLACKIE
> (to Burley, heartily)
I'll *love* it!

At which point o.s. the Professor, unaccompanied by the orchestra, starts to play on the PIANO the introduction to "A Heart That Is Free." Blackie looks quizzically off toward the Professor.

ORCHESTRA PIT   PROFESSOR   BLACKIE'S POV
The Professor, coming to the end of the introduction, looks up at the stage, tossing a look of encouragement toward the wings.

STAGE   PROFESSOR'S POV
MARY COMES OUT—excited—yet diffident and starts to SING.

She sings a little way when:

ORCHESTRA PIT   PROFESSOR
The Professor looks from Mary over toward Baldini.

BLACKIE'S BOX   BLACKIE   BALDINI   BURLEY   PROFESSOR'S
POV
Baldini and Burley are looking off at Mary in interest. Blackie is
watching her, covering his annoyance at the breach of show-
manship with a smile.

STAGE   MARY   BLACKIE'S POV
Mary is SINGING a particularly brilliant passage.

BLACKIE'S BOX   BLACKIE   BALDINI   BURLEY
Burley turns to Baldini, beginning to be excited over Mary.

> BURLEY
> That girl *has* got a voice!

> BALDINI
> (enthusiastic)
> A voice, indeed! And she's had training, too!

Burley is beaming and feasting his eyes on Mary.

> BURLEY
> Yes!

Blackie looks at Burley, studying him as he looks at Mary in
increasing delight—fairly eating her up with his eyes.

STAGE   MARY   BURLEY'S POV
Mary is SINGING on, brilliantly.

BLACKIE'S BOX   BLACKIE   BURLEY   BALDINI
Mary continues the song, Burley and Baldini watching her in
delight, and Blackie watching Burley—smiling as if amused at
his reaction to Mary. Presently, MAT crashes into the box.

> MAT
> (irate—bursting out)
> Look here, Boss—are you gonna let that crazy dame
> horse this show around and—

Baldini turns to Mat and puts his finger at his mouth in a gesture
of silence.

                      BALDINI

Sh!

Mat looks at Baldini, surprised at being shushed. Blackie responds by being overly hospitable toward the wishes of his guests.

                      BLACKIE

Never mind, Mat.

                      MAT
                  (protesting)

But, Blackie! I—

                      BLACKIE

Let it go. Forget it.

Mat stands a moment, registering his surprise at Blackie and his distaste of Mary, then turns and LEAVES.

STAGE MARY

Mary reaches the end of the SONG, attains a brilliant high note, and GOES ON OFF.

BLACKIE'S BOX BLACKIE   BURLEY   BALDINI

Burley and Baldini are APPLAUDING.

               BURLEY AND BALDINI

Brava! Brava!

Blackie looks off toward the audience.

THE AUDIENCE BLACKIE'S POV

Most of the audience is paying no attention to what they've heard—but a few scattered customers of a higher type are APPLAUDING.

BLACKIE'S BOX BLACKIE   BURLEY   BALDINI

Burley turns to Blackie and smiles affably.

                    BURLEY

How long has this girl been down here?

Blackie smiles at Burley and settles back at ease.

                      BLACKIE

Just started.

BURLEY
Really? What's her name?

The PROFESSOR excitedly barges up to the rail of the box just in time to hear the above question.

PROFESSOR
(to Burley)
Mary Blake!
(to Baldini)
What did I tell you, Maestro! Was I wrong or was I—

BLACKIE
(cutting in, amusedly)
Will you get back to that piano?

PROFESSOR
Yes, Mr. Norton.

Professor starts—then turns.

PROFESSOR (cont'd)
I don't care if you fire me. At least I've had the opportunity to help a great—

BLACKIE
(amused)
Who said I was firing you? Get going.

PROFESSOR
(delighted, relieved)
Sure! Sure! Thank you! Sure!

The PROFESSOR GOES OFF.

BURLEY
(to Blackie—with enthusiasm)
I'd like to meet this girl!

Burley turns—calls a passing WAITER.

BURLEY (cont'd)
Oh, waiter.

The waiter steps up to the box.

WAITER
Yes, Mr. Burley.

Burley smiles in anticipation, takes out his pocketbook, and removes a card.

> BURLEY
> Will you ask Miss Blake if she'll meet a respectful admirer?

The waiter takes the card.

> WAITER
> Yes, sir!

The WAITER LEAVES. Blackie smiles at what he considers a sucker move on Burley's part. He turns to Burley.

> BLACKIE
> I haven't had her working the boxes yet, Burley.

> BURLEY
> (chuckles)
> I'm glad of that.
> (to Baldini)
> One never knows where one is going to find talent.

Blackie smiles.

> BLACKIE
> (kidding Burley)
> No. One never does, does one?

Baldini thinks Blackie's remark is on the level.

> BALDINI
> (enthusiastic)
> To quote from Plautus:—"*Saepe summa ingenia in occulto latent.*"

> BLACKIE
> (chuckling)
> You took the words right out of my mouth!

At which point the door of the box opens and MARY ENTERS, her stage costume covered by a long cape. Burley and Baldini rise. Blackie remains seated. Mary looks at Burley.

> MARY
> (diffident, yet excited)

Mr. Burley?
Burley, on the make, takes her hand with great gallantry.

> BURLEY
> It's very gracious of you to allow us this privilege, Miss
> Blake.

Blackie smiles at Burley's technique.

> MARY
> Oh, thanks.

> BURLEY
> May I present Signor Baldini?

> MARY
> How do you do, Signor.

> BALDINI
> Good evening, my dear.

Baldini kisses her hand—Blackie watching him criticizingly.
Never taking his delighted gaze off Mary, Burley pulls out a
chair.

> BURLEY
> Won't you sit down?

Mary sits.

> BALDINI
> (excitedly)
> Hearing a voice like yours in a variety theatre has been
> a real experience.

> MARY
> Thank you.

She begins to take heart a little.

> MARY (cont'd)
> But I sat in your outer office at the Tivoli once—for six
> days.

> BALDINI
> Really?

> BURLEY
> (to Baldini, laughing loudly)

I'm going to see that the Board of Directors hears of that!
Baldini LAUGHS. Burley again looks Mary over delightedly.

> BURLEY (cont'd)
> So—you want to sing in opera?

> MARY
> That's why I came to San Francisco.

Blackie watches Burley, amused at what he considers 'sucker'
technique.

> BALDINI
> You've had training, haven't you?

Mary begins to get excited.

> MARY
> From the best teacher in Denver. I led the Bach Choral
> Society! And won first prize in the Schubert Festival—
> and I've learned Marguerite and Mimi and Violetta and
> Puccini's *Butterfly*. I love Puccini!

Baldini kisses his fingers and:

> BALDINI
> (in ecstasy)
> Ah—Puccini!

Blackie smiles. Burley CHUCKLES to Blackie—then taking a
crack at his lack of culture:

> BURLEY
> Ever hear of Puccini, Norton?

> BLACKIE
> (grinning)
> Didn't he run a joint on Dupont Street?

They smile. Burley once more looks Mary over with delight.

> BURLEY
> Well—after all, there's no law against an opera singer
> being slender and young and beautiful.

Blackie looks at him with a superior smile.

> BURLEY (cont'd)
> (to Baldini)

What do you think of giving Miss Blake an audition?

BALDINI
I think by all means—yes.
Mary is thrilled—overcome—almost unable to believe it.

BLACKIE
(as if deeply sincere)
It's darn sweet of you, Burley—taking an interest in this little lady. And you too, Signor. But unfortunately she's under a two-year contract.

BURLEY
To whom?

BLACKIE
(as if really regretful)
To me.
Mary shoots a look of keen disappointment at Blackie. Baldini looks at Blackie, then:

BALDINI
(regretfully)
Two years!
CHUCKLING over his victory,

BLACKIE
(to Burley)
But I'll have her send you word when it runs out.

BURLEY
Surely you wouldn't let *that* stand in Miss Blake's way of a chance to sing at the Tivoli?

BLACKIE
(smugly, enjoying himself)
She's doing *all right* here.
Burley gives Blackie a long, smilingly contemptuous glance. Then, shrugging his shoulders at Mary,

BURLEY
I'm sorry, Miss Blake.
Mary is trying hard to keep back the tears.

MARY

Mr. Norton's right!

Blackie looks sharply up at her.

MARY (cont'd)

The Paradise is just as important to him as the Tivoli is
to you.

Blackie wears a smug look.

MARY (cont'd)
(to Baldini)

What would happen to the Tivoli if you let your artists
walk out any time they wished?

BALDINI
(warmly—admiringly)

You're very loyal, Miss Blake.

MARY
(to Baldini)

I'm very grateful to Mr. Norton.

Blackie swells up and grins at his victory being completed. Mary
is still choking back her keen disappointment.

MARY
(simply)

I'm afraid I'll have to go.

As she rises,

MARY

We don't have much time between numbers.
(to Baldini)

Good-bye, Signor. You've made this the happiest night
of my life.

BALDINI

Thank you, my dear.

Baldini kisses her hand.

MARY
(to Burley)

Good-bye.

BURLEY

Good night.

Burley takes her hand—warmly gallant—giving her the works.

BURLEY (cont'd)

I haven't given up yet—about the Tivoli.

Mary smiles—with just a touch of bitterness.

MARY

I'm afraid you don't know Mr. Norton.

BURLEY

You don't know *me*!

Burley raises her hand with gallantry and charm, kisses it, Blackie watching, amused at his technique. As Mary turns to go, Blackie rises.

BLACKIE

(to Mary—smiling)

Oh—wait a moment.

Mary stops. Blackie moves aside with her. For one brief second his iron will breaks through his smiling exterior and he becomes brutally direct:

BLACKIE (cont'd)

Well—now that you've made your impression, don't sing that highbrow number again.

As she looks up at him in fright, he suddenly smiles, his very smile and quietness revealing his inner strength and assurance.

BLACKIE (cont'd)

I don't like those things.

Saying which, Blackie gives her cheek a little pinch. Mary looks at him, tears in her eyes, turns and starts to go.

BLACKIE (cont'd)

(matter-of-factly)

Oh, wait.

Blackie looks at his watch.

BLACKIE (cont'd)

(casually)

A friend of mine runs a joint around on Kearny Street. I want you to hurry over there and tear off a little number for him.

> MARY
> (dejectedly)
> Yes. Where is it?

> BLACKIE
> (lightly)
> Saint Anne's Mission just around the corner.

Mary looks up sharply.

> MARY
> (amazed)
> Saint Anne's—

> BLACKIE
> Yeah. Ask for Father Mullin.

Blackie smiles.

> BLACKIE (cont'd)
> (amusedly—tolerantly)
> I guess you know all that hokey-pokey they sing in those traps.

Mary stands looking—just looking.

> BLACKIE (cont'd)
> (briskly—yet kindly)
> You've got a number to do back here at ten thirty. Get going.

Mary pulls herself up out of her mood of amazement and GOES. Blackie looks after her a moment—then goes back to his seat in the box.

> BLACKIE
> (to Burley—with sarcasm)
> So *you* don't want me to run for City Supervisor?

> BURLEY
> You know as well as I it isn't practical to rebuild the Coast, Norton.

BLACKIE

Why not?

BURLEY

The Coast is picturesque. Folks come down here slum-
ming! They don't want to feel they're in a "Spotless
Town!"

BLACKIE

That isn't your reason, Burley.

BURLEY

It's one of them.

BLACKIE

Yeah—but the main one is that you don't want to *spend
your dough* to make your property down here safe.

BURLEY

If I did what you wanted to my property it would be a
calamity for the Coast!

BLACKIE

(sarcastically)

How do you figure that?

BURLEY

The Burley estate has to get a certain interest on its investment. I'd have to raise rents. You boys couldn't
live! You'd be forced to charge ten cents for a glass of
beer.

Blackie studies Burley for a moment, then:

BLACKIE

(to Baldini)

I don't quite get him, Mr. Baldini. He tosses a fortune
every year into the Tivoli Opera House.

Smiling, Baldini shrugs his shoulders.

BURLEY

(to Blackie)

That's not business. That's for *Frisco*.

BLACKIE
(warmly)
The Coast is Frisco, too!

BURLEY
(just as warmly)
That's why I wouldn't change it!
Blackie pauses, then:

BLACKIE
(with finality)
Well—Burley—these little mugs down here are *my* people. And I'm going to see that they get a square deal.
BABE ENTERS the box.

BLACKIE (cont'd)
So I'm not pulling out of this fight.
Burley rises and:

BURLEY
(with finality)
All right, Norton. I didn't want to fight you—but if you're asking for it—
Burley shrugs his shoulders.

BLACKIE
Go ahead.

BURLEY
(simply—in conversational tone)
Good night.

BLACKIE
(same tone)
Good night.
(to Baldini)
Good night, Baldini.

BALDINI
Good night.
BURLEY and BALDINI GO ON OUT.

                         BABE
                     (to Blackie)
            You're wanted on the phone.
Blackie heads for the telephone on the side wall in a recess back
of his box.

                        BLACKIE
                      (in phone)
            Hello.
A broad grin overspreads Blackie's face.

                     BLACKIE (cont'd)
            Oh, hello, Tim.

INT   OFFICE OF CHAPEL   TIM
The office is in a Barbary Coast Rescue Mission. Tim, dressed in
his long black ecclesiastical robe, is at the phone. O.s. there is
ORGAN MUSIC.

                          TIM
            Well, kid—you've given us all a big night over here.
            I've just finished the service so why don't you come on
            over?

BLACKIE'S BOX   BLACKIE
Blackie, on the phone, grins quizzically.

                        BLACKIE
            What for?
O.s. we hear the HOT RHYTHM MUSIC of the Paradise.

CHAPEL OFFICE   TIM
Tim, on the phone.

                          TIM
            For the organ recital and to hear the young lady sing.

BLACKIE'S BOX   BLACKIE
Blackie, on the phone.

                        BLACKIE
            She'll be coming back here . . . to sing the things I *like*!

CHAPEL OFFICE   TIM
Tim, on the phone.

> TIM

All right. Have it your own way. I was just sort of hoping you'd make my evening complete. If I had you over here I'd hug you and then I'd knock your block off. But I guess I don't have to tell you again how I feel about the organ.

BLACKIE'S BOX   BLACKIE
Blackie, on the phone.

> BLACKIE

Aw—forget it!
And Blackie LAUGHS it off.

CHAPEL OFFICE   TIM
Tim, on the phone.

> TIM

All right, Blackie . . . Good-bye.
Tim hangs up the phone and goes to the door. He opens the door.

CHAPEL   TIM
From the open door Tim looks into the church where we see a crowd of derelicts of the Coast seated. MARY stands at the organ, her stage costume covered by a long cape, waiting. Tim gives a signal to the ORGANIST who begins to play the introduction to "In a Monastery Garden." Mary begins to SING. Tim watches Mary, moved by the spirituality of her beauty as she sings. He looks over the congregation. We see various types of derelicts listening, deeply affected, to Mary's song. Tim turns from the derelicts to Mary—studying her. Mary is SINGING, her face transfigured by the spirit of the song. She finally FINISHES THE SONG and turns to go. The organist continues to PLAY A SOLO. Several of the derelicts rise and start to go out. Tim moves down to the chapel door to meet them. The derelicts at the door include a RAGGED OLD MAN and TWO PAINTED GIRLS.

> RAGGED OLD MAN
> (to Tim)
> Good night, Father!

TIM
Good night, Mike. Have you got any money?

RAGGED OLD MAN
(grinning)
Sure. Me wife's got a job.

TWO PAINTED GIRLS
(in unison)
Good night, Father.

TIM
Good night. Can you get home all right?

TWO PAINTED GIRLS
Sure. Oh, sure.
Mary now reaches the door as the RAGGED OLD MAN and the
TWO PAINTED GIRLS EXIT.

MARY
Good night, Father Mullin.
Tim, anxious to know something about her, detains her.

TIM
It was pretty nice of you to leave your work and come
to our rescue.

MARY
(smiling)
It's made me feel good—being here.

TIM
You're not the girl whose father was a preacher?

MARY
(surprised)
Yes. How did you know?
Tim studies her and:

TIM
Blackie Norton told me.
Tim gestures off toward the vestry door.

TIM (cont'd)
Come on in here—I'd like to talk to you.

MARY
I'm afraid I'll be late.
As he leads her toward the vestry door,

TIM
That's all right—I'll fix it with Blackie.
Tim opens the door and ushers her in.

CHAPEL OFFICE   MARY   TIM
The office is very neat—colorful—attractive. On a small iron
stove a pot of water is boiling cosily. Tim leads Mary in and
closes the door. O.s. the MUSIC of the ORGAN continues
throughout the scene. Tim places a chair for Mary.

TIM
Sit down, won't you?

MARY
Thank you.
Mary sits.

TIM
How are you making out at the Paradise?
Trying to cover her distaste for the Paradise,

MARY
(evasively)
Well—I've only just started.

TIM
I see.
Tim goes to a little cupboard and opens it, revealing an array of
paraphernalia for making and serving coffee neatly arranged—
the coffee in a striped paper bag.

TIM (cont'd)
Will you join me in a cup?

MARY
Thanks.

As he proceeds to make coffee—using boiling water from the kettle on the stove,

> TIM
>
> How d'you like Blackie?

> MARY
>
> (frankly)
> I'm afraid of him.

> TIM
>
> And he's someone to be afraid of!

Mary looks up sharply.

> TIM (cont'd)
>
> He's as unscrupulous with women as he is ruthless with men.

As she looks at Tim,

> MARY
>
> Why did he send me *here*? I don't understand him.

Tim LAUGHS.

> TIM
>
> You probably understand him a whole lot better than he understands you.

Mary looks questioningly at him.

> TIM (cont'd)
>
> You see—I don't think Blackie ever knew your kind of woman before. But you needn't be afraid of him unless . . . you're afraid of yourself.

Tim looks at her.

> TIM (cont'd)
>
> Are you?

Mary hesitates just a second as this new thought strikes her—then:

> MARY
>
> No.

Mary smiles.

MARY (cont'd)

I guess I'm a little bit dazed. You see, I've been in San Francisco for six weeks and nothing has happened at all. Then—in the past twenty-four hours—the whole world went topsy-turvy. I feel like running home.

TIM

If you *are* afraid—you'd better run home.

Mary looks up at him. There's a pause.

TIM (cont'd)

How about it?

MARY

(smiling)

I'm going to stay.

TIM

(in approval)

That's right!

There's a PAUSE as he finishes putting the coffee on to boil. Then, turning to Mary,

TIM

You're in probably the wickedest, most corrupt, most Godless city in America. Sometimes it frightens *me* and I wonder what the end is going to be. But nothing can harm you if you don't allow it to. Because nothing in the world—*no one* in the world is *all* bad!

Tim gestures toward the Chapel.

TIM (cont'd)

Do you know who gave the Chapel the new organ we've been dedicating tonight?

MARY

No.

TIM

The most Godless and scoffing and unbelieving soul in all San Francisco.

Mary looks up.

TIM (cont'd)

. . . Blackie Norton.

Mary stares at him—just stares. As Tim starts to get cups, etc. for serving coffee, he smiles in reminiscence.

TIM (cont'd)

Blackie heard one night that I was saving for an organ. The very next morning some men arrived here to plan the installation. It cost him four thousand dollars!

He smiles.

TIM (cont'd)

If he'd save his money for two weeks, he'd be a rich man.

Tim turns to face Mary who has never removed her gaze from him.

TIM (cont'd)

He's a tremendous force, Blackie is. If he'd only be a force for good instead of evil. I've tried to do something with him for years but I've never had any luck. Maybe I'm not the right one.

Tim looks at her. A PAUSE as Mary looks back at him. Then—

MARY

You've known him a long time, haven't you?

TIM

Sure.

He smiles in reminiscence.

TIM (cont'd)

Blackie and I were kids together—born and brought up on the Coast. We used to sell newspapers in the joints along Pacific Street. Blackie was the leader of all the kids in the neighborhood. And I was his *pal*!

Tim CHUCKLES in affectionate reminiscence.

TIM (cont'd)

Our families used to try and make us go to Sunday school. We generally ducked—but the time came that I *wanted* to go. And Blackie thought I was crazy.

A thoughtful PAUSE as Mary looks at him, then—

> TIM
>
> When I made up my mind I was going to study for the Priesthood I wanted to *talk* to Blackie about it—see if I couldn't get him to understand—to feel a little as I felt. But he just said "Good luck, sucker." And that was all.

Tim PAUSES. He SIGHS.

> TIM (cont'd)
>
> We've never been able to have that talk. I came back from Santa Clara College and found Blackie deeper than ever in the life of the Coast. And he's gone right on. But he has a sort of code. He's always had—from the time he was a kid. He never lied—he never cheated and he never took an underhanded advantage of anyone.

Tim rises and goes to a desk. There he picks up a small framed picture.

> TIM (cont'd)
>
> Here we are, the two of us when we were kids.

Tim hands Mary the picture. She looks at it. Tim LAUGHS.

> TIM (cont'd)
>
> Don't let him know I told you about that organ. He'd never forgive me.

> MARY
>
> I won't.

Mary looks at the photograph in her hand.

> TIM
>
> Blackie's that way—ashamed of his *good deeds* as other people are ashamed of their sins.

Mary studies the photograph.

INSERT SHOT PHOTOGRAPH
It shows the boys at the age of about twelve standing in front of a saloon—their newspapers in one arm—their other arms about each other's shoulders.

TIM (OS)

But nobody will ever convince me that there's not a whole lot more good than there is bad in Blackie Norton.

FADE OUT:

During the FADE the o.s. ORGAN MUSIC changes to that of a raucous BRASS BAND playing "San Francisco."

FADE IN:

EXT   CLOSE SHOT   SCHUTZEN PARK   BANNER   DAY

At first all we see is a picture of Blackie on a banner reading:

FOR CITY SUPERVISOR
BLACKIE NORTON
BORN AND RAISED ON
THE BARBARY COAST

During the MUSIC, the CAMERA PULLS BACK, revealing a platform in Schutzen Park (a beer garden across the bay from San Francisco). Seated about on the platform are ALASKA, RED KELLY, GUS, and CHICK dressed in their best and wearing Blackie Norton badges. BLACKIE is seated at one side trying not to look self-conscious. In the center of the platform, seated at a little table, is the chairman, JOE KINKO. Kinko has been a prize-fight announcer and his movements and gestures during the occasion are those of the prize ring. As "San Francisco" comes to its close, the band goes into *"Acht du Lieber Augustine"* and MAT jumps up onto the stage to lead the audience in the campaign song:

MAT

(singing)

We're all for *Blackie Norton*
Blackie Norton, Blackie Norton
We're all for *Blackie Norton*
The King of the Coast!

He is the people's choice
That's why we raise our voice

All for *Blackie Norton*
The King of the Coast!
During the song we see various Coast types seated about, all dressed up, wearing badges and SINGING lustily. BABE goes up to a fellow who is not singing.

BABE

(with menace)

Why ain't you singin'?

The man looks up at Babe, sees his expression and instantly starts to SING. Meanwhile, Blackie looking off sees something which apparently interests and surprises him. He sees MARY seated in the crowd, interested and taking everything in. Beside her sits the PROFESSOR. Blackie swells up—smiles to himself, turns and becomes absorbed in the proceedings. The SONG ENDS. The crowd breaks into LOUD APPLAUSE and CHEERING. Kinko steps forward on the stage—and—in the manner of the prize ring—holds up his hands for silence. The crowd QUIETS DOWN. In his best ring manner,

KINKO
(yelling at the top of his voice)
Ladies and *gentlemen*! Introducing the *President* of the
Ladies' Blackie Norton Club, Miss *Della* . . .
With a violent pointing of the finger to one side:

KINKO (cont'd)
Bailey!
There's LOUD APPLAUSE as DELLA, seated to the extreme side,
rises and acknowledges the applause. Della is dressed to the
nines and wears across her ample bosom a ribbon on which is
printed "BLACKIE NORTON—OUR CHOICE." Della addresses
the crowd:

DELLA
Girls and boys—I just want to tell you that the ladies of
the Coast wish to go on record as endorsin' Blackie
Norton right up to the limit.
Della sits down. The crowd APPLAUDS.

GIRLS IN CROWD
That's right, Della!
You said it!
We're all for Blackie!
Kinko holds up his hand for silence—then—

KINKO
(at top of his voice)
Ladies and gentlemen! I want to introduce that great
guy, *our candidate*—born on the Coast—raised on the
Coast—*lives* on the Coast—our *champion*, Blackie—
Again with a violent pointing of his finger:

KINKO (cont'd)
NORTON!
Blackie grins and rises. The crowd APPLAUDS. As the
APPLAUSE is dying down,

BLACKIE
(very cocky)
Thanks.
The APPLAUSE now CEASES.

BLACKIE (cont'd)
I'm no politician—I didn't ask for this, but now that I'm
in it, I'm not going to stop till I get some decent fire
laws for our people down on the Coast!
LOUD APPLAUSE. HAZELTINE, a big tough-looking mug seated
down front, rises.

HAZELTINE
Wait a minute, Norton! What I'd like to know is what
construction company is payin' you for tryin' to rebuild
the Coast?
Blackie looks at him.
ANOTHER HECKLER hops up from the crowd.

ANOTHER HECKLER
Yeah! That's right! How about it, Blackie?
A few in the crowd MURMUR APPROVAL.

HAZELTINE
Why are you going into politics, Norton? Go on! Tell
us!
Blackie jumps down off the platform.

BLACKIE
Here's an answer you can take to your *boss*—Jack Burley!
The crowd REACTS to mention of Burley's name. Hazeltine
starts to defend himself but Blackie beats him to it, landing a
brutal sock on his chin. Hazeltine stands as if paralyzed. Blackie
jumps back on the platform, going right on with the speech as if
never having been interrupted.

BLACKIE
(sore, earnest, vehement)
We've tried long enough to get a square deal from a lot
of pot-bellied land owners up on Nob Hill—now we're
going to go after it on our own!
APPLAUSE. Blackie, looking down, spots a red-headed, freckle
faced KID with both hands in dirty bandages. He is standing
right in front of the platform. Grabbing the kid by the coat collar,

Blackie jerks him up on the platform—the kid surprised. As he points to the kid,

> BLACKIE (cont'd)
>
> This is Jim Sullivan's kid. Last New Year's Eve he and his sister had to jump two floors out of a burning building.

There's a MURMUR of indignation from the crowd and voices call: "That's right, Blackie!" You're darn tootin'." The kid swells all up, grinning with pleasure over the attention he's getting. The crowd LAUGHS. Blackie, grinning in amusement at the kid, playfully gives him a little spank, starting him on his way off the platform. Blackie once more becomes deadly serious.

> BLACKIE
>
> (to crowd)
>
> Are we going to go on—letting these Nob Hill stiffs make *fire dancers* out of our women and kids? Not if I can help it!

There's wild, unanimous APPLAUSE and CRIES of "No!" "You bet we ain't!" "We're with you, Blackie!" Pleased at their reaction, Blackie grins, his mood changing to one of whole-hearted fun.

> BLACKIE
>
> And now, free beer on me!

He jumps down off the platform, turns to head out toward where Mary is sitting, but is cut off by TRIXIE coming up.

> TRIXIE
>
> Gee kiddo—you were swell!

Trixie starts to take his arm.

> TRIXIE (cont'd)
>
> I'm so proud of you I could—

> BLACKIE
>
> (cutting in)
>
> Thanks. You run along and get yourself some beer.

> TRIXIE
>
> (deeply disappointed)

But Blackie—aren't we going to be together?

BLACKIE
I told you I'd be busy when I brought you out here.

TRIXIE
Where'll I wait for you?
Anxious to get rid of her,

BLACKIE
By that first beer truck over there. Get yourself a drink.
That's the girl!
He gives her a pat and heads straight for where he saw Mary. As
Blackie makes his way through the crowd, different types call off
to him right and left. They hold out their beer glasses and:

PEOPLE IN CROWD
Here's to you, Blackie!
Here's how!
Best of luck!
We're all with you, Blackie!
Blackie salutes right and left in answer to their greetings. He
reaches the table where Mary sits. The Professor is just coming
up with two glasses of beer. As if not noting Mary's presence,

BLACKIE
Professor!
The Professor looks up.

BLACKIE (cont'd)
Will you do a little errand for me?

PROFESSOR
Why, yes.

BLACKIE
I'd like you to get Trixie and take her back to town.

PROFESSOR
To town?

BLACKIE
Yeah.
                    (sotto voce—out of the side of his mouth)

She's hanging around those beer trucks—getting stiff.

                    PROFESSOR
Oh . . . but what about Miss Blake?
Blackie is about to go, then stops.

                    BLACKIE
Huh?
Then, as if just noticing Mary,

                    BLACKIE (cont'd)
Oh. How d'you do.

                    MARY
          (simply)
How do you do.

                    PROFESSOR
I brought Miss Blake out here and I—

                    BLACKIE
          (to Professor)
I'll see that she gets home.
          (to Mary)
     Stick around!
Mary is thrilled in spite of herself—catches her breath and looks
sharply up at him. O.s. DANCE MUSIC starts.

BEER AREA   HAZELTINE
Hazeltine, now partly recovered, stands just about to raise a
glass of beer to his mouth. BLACKIE ENTERS the scene, sees
Hazeltine and stops. He reaches out, puts a hand on Hazeltine's
arm and brings it slowly down, Hazeltine frightened as the beer
retreats from his mouth.

                    BLACKIE
     Not *my* beer!
At which Blackie nonchalantly socks him (a short-arm sock) and
EXITS, LAUGHING, from the scene. Hazeltine stands dazed by
the LAUGHING CROWD in b.g. A dazed, goofy expression
comes over his face. As he slowly sinks OUT OF FRAME,
                              DISSOLVE TO:

DANCE FLOOR   BLACKIE   MARY

On the open air dance floor at Schutzen Park, Blackie and Mary are dancing to the MUSIC of "Would You." Mary is looking off, self-conscious, frightened at the tremendous attraction she feels for Blackie, holding in to keep from succumbing to it. Blackie, heartily and boyishly enjoying himself, is looking down at Mary, taking her all in, unconscious of her fears. Presently, Blackie, becoming conscious of the tune, listens to it. Finally:

BLACKIE

That's awfully pretty—Know the name of it?

MARY

"Would you."
Blackie grins ingratiatingly.

BLACKIE

(amused)

Would you what?

Mary becomes confused, unable to answer. They dance a moment longer, Blackie smiling at her—then presently looking off, amused, he directs her attention toward what he sees. They look over and see a WOMAN dancing with a POT-BELLIED MAN who is so fat he has to hold her at arms' length. The woman, however, has managed, by straining, to get her head to the man's chest where she rests it in delirious joy, her eyes closed. Presently the man, looking off, sees Blackie.

POT-BELLIED MAN
(grinning)
Hello, Blackie.

Mary looks off at the fat man. Blackie, still grinning, salutes the man in answer, looks down at Mary, and they LAUGH together. Blackie suddenly pulls Mary close and pulls *her* head down to *his* chest. Her smile fades. She looks worried as he holds her tight. She is uncomfortable for a moment, but presently, in spite of herself, she begins to succumb, giving in to the mood of the music. They dance a moment longer, and suddenly bump into a MAN and WOMAN, the woman dancing with a baby thrown over her shoulder.

MAN
Excuse me, Blackie.

Blackie, grinning, nods in response. He and Mary are now dancing near the edge of the dance floor where a man, standing by a refreshment counter, is just putting mustard on a hot dog. As he turns to put down the mustard spoon, Blackie neatly removes the sandwich from his hand, going right on dancing. Mary LAUGHS as Blackie takes a big bite of the sandwich. Blackie, his mouth full, LAUGHS and offers her a bite. She takes one, and LAUGHING, they continue to dance in closer accord than they have ever been.

DISSOLVE TO:

LONG SHOT   COUNTRY ROAD   BLACKIE'S TRAP
Blackie's trap goes over a lovely country road.

DISSOLVE TO:

BLACKIE'S TRAP   BLACKIE   MARY
Blackie, driving expertly with one hand, is looking straight

ahead at the horses. Mary, leaning back, is tired after a full day.
She is also looking straight ahead—thoughtful—knowing herself tempted and in danger, knowing that Blackie is going to
make love to her. They drive a little while in SILENCE. Finally
Blackie turns his gaze on her, looking her over in satisfaction,
fairly eating her up. Mary, not even looking up at him, senses
that his gaze is on her. Uncomfortably she looks off in the oppo-
site direction. Blackie smiles and:

> BLACKIE
> (with seduction)
> Glad you came?

Mary hesitates, trying to gain her composure. Diffident—uncomfortable—she turns her face—looks up at him, giving a
forced smile in answer, and then, unable to stand his gaze,
again looks away. Blackie's gaze never leaves her.

> BLACKIE
> (puzzled)
> What's the matter?

Mary PAUSES—then—trying hard to be composed:

> MARY
> Nothing.

They go on a little while in SILENCE. Blackie driving slowly,
which we sense by the o.s. HOOF BEATS of the HORSES. Blackie
studies her, amused, puzzled—Mary thinking hard, trying to
find a subject to lead him out of his present mood. Finally Blackie reaches over and puts his free arm back of her on the top of
the carriage seat. Mary is frightened by the thrill she feels at his
gesture—nervously—with a forced smile:

> MARY
> Would you mind driving a little faster? I . . . I prom-
> ised Father Mullin I'd stop in if I had time.

Blackie removes his arm from behind her.

> BLACKIE
> (quizzically agreeable)
> All right.

Blackie whips up the horse.

                    BLACKIE (cont'd)
Step along there, Betsy.

LONG SHOT   BLACKIE'S TRAP   BLACKIE   MARY
Blackie flicks the horses—they speed up.

BLACKIE'S TRAP   BLACKIE   MARY
The background quickens for a moment.

                    BLACKIE
                (amused)
You and Tim seem to be hitting it off pretty well.

                    MARY
                (constrained)
Yes.

                    BLACKIE
                (with amused curiosity)
What d'you talk about?

                    MARY
                (still constrained)
Oh, lots of things . . . his work.
Blackie LAUGHS.

                    BLACKIE
That's right—you believe in that hocus-pocus, don't you?

                    MARY
Yes.
Putting up a pathetic attempt to reach his better nature,

                    MARY (cont'd)
                (warmly)
Even if I hadn't believed—the faith of a man like Father Mullin would have made me.
Blackie looks at her regretfully.

                    BLACKIE
That's the trouble.
Blackie hits her on the knee.

> BLACKIE (cont'd)
> It gets people who are *all right* and makes monkeys out of 'em. It *lost me* Tim Mullin!
> (warmly)
> He'd have made the greatest gambler the Coast ever had—the only mug I ever wanted to hang onto!

They drive on a little in SILENCE except for the o.s. HOOF BEATS. Again in effort to reach his better nature,

> MARY
> (quietly, sincerely)
> He loves you more than anyone else in the world.

> BLACKIE
> (bitterly sarcastic)
> Yeah? Well—he blew me for a lot of plaster saints!

As he moves closer to her,

> BLACKIE (cont'd)
> (insinuatingly, almost with warning)
> I don't go for that sort of sucker competition . . . Mary.

This is the first time he calls her by her first name.

> BLACKIE (cont'd)
> Blackie's got to be number one boy.

In what is in reality a love speech:

> MARY
> (pleadingly)
> It isn't competition! I think that people who believe in something can love each other more!

> BLACKIE
> (amusedly—tolerantly—as to a child)
> Well, honey, if that's what you believe—it's all right with me. I don't hold it against you.

He starts to put his arm around back of her. Frightened at the thrill she gets from his gesture, she pulls away. Surprised at her rebuff, Blackie removes his arm—studies her a moment. Finally—

BLACKIE
(with honest curiosity)
Who's the mug you're stuck on?

MARY
Nobody.
Blackie's gaze never leaves her.

BLACKIE
Didn't there *used* to be one?

MARY
No.
Blackie begins to be amazed.

BLACKIE
Never?

MARY
No.
Blackie gives in to utter amazement. He pulls up the horses.

BLACKIE
WHOA!

LONG SHOT   BLACKIE'S TRAP
We see the carriage suddenly stop.

CLOSE SHOT   BLACKIE'S TRAP   BLACKIE   MARY
Blackie looks Mary over in whole-hearted stupefaction.

BLACKIE
Are you kidding?
She looks at him—just looks. Blackie PAUSES—finally:

BLACKIE (cont'd)
Well, I'm a sucker if I ever knew a girl like you before!
Giddap!
O.s. HOOF BEATS begin as carriage starts.

LONG SHOT   BLACKIE'S TRAP
We see the carriage as he starts the team.

BLACKIE'S TRAP   BLACKIE   MARY
Blackie is highly amused and CHUCKLES.

BLACKIE

You must have used some pretty clever foot work to side-step those dudes out in Benson, Colorado.

Mary PAUSES as she struggles to assume a light manner to cover up her inward feelings.

MARY

It wasn't so difficult, Mr. Norton.

Blackie nudges her.

BLACKIE
(insinuatingly charming, correcting her)
Blackie!

Mary looks up at him—hesitates a moment—then:

MARY
(softly, falteringly)
Blackie.

BLACKIE
(relieved—with satisfaction)
That's better!

Saying which, he reaches over and puts his arm around her. This time Mary, powerless against the terrific effect he has on her, does not withdraw. He pulls her closer. She looks straight ahead as they drive on.

FADE OUT.

FADE IN:

EXT FOUNDERS CLUB

The Founders Club is a large, luxuriously substantial building with the name carved in the stone above the entrance.

DISSOLVE TO:

INT CLUB ROOM

In a luxurious room of the club seated about the fire in the enormous fireplace are four imposing-looking, middle-aged men, in attitudes of luxurious relaxation. One, a MAN WITH PAPER, asleep and gently SNORING, is holding a newspaper over his face—on one finger an enormous diamond ring. Two others are lazily engaged in a game of dominoes, FIRST DOMINO PLAYER

and A DEAF MAN, his partner in the game. A MAN WITH
COFFEE is being served with coffee by a very pompous BUTLER.
BURLEY ENTERS the scene briskly and takes a stand directly in
front of the fire. The others, preoccupied and lazy, pay no attention to him. Burley looks them all over—then—briskly—
rubbing his hands:

> BURLEY
> You boys better see a heart specialist. This excitement's
> going to get you.

They all continue their occupations, paying no attention to this
crack for a moment. But presently, the man with the paper over
his face CEASES SNORING and removes the paper.

> MAN WITH PAPER
> (partly in reprimand)
> Say, Burley—that fellow Blackie Norton is going to
> raise Cain if he gets onto the Board of Supervisors.

Making a play,

> FIRST DOMINO PLAYER
> He sure will!

> DEAF MAN
> Who's that?

> FIRST DOMINO PLAYER
> Norton.

> DEAF MAN
> Oh.

Burley, smiling assuredly, lights a cigarette.

> MAN WITH COFFEE
> (continuing the reprimand)
> You know, Burley, *you* aren't the *only one* that's got
> property on the Coast! If Norton wins that election it's
> going to cost us *all* plenty!

> BURLEY
> I know how to put the damper on him.

MAN WITH PAPER

Well, you'd better get going. If there's another big fire down there and a lot of lives lost they're going to blame us.

BURLEY

No they won't! We'll call it an act of God.

All but the deaf man LAUGH uproariously.

DEAF MAN

What's that?

MAN WITH PAPER

(still laughing)

Act of God!

The deaf man joins in the LAUGHTER. Burley starts out.

DISSOLVE TO:

EXT   FRONT OF PARADISE

It's about 11:30 A.M. O.s. we hear the ORCHESTRA rehearsing "The One I Love" accompanied by MARY SINGING. BURLEY ENTERS the shot from street and goes into the Paradise.

INT   PARADISE AUDITORIUM   PROFESSOR   MAT   OTHERS

The auditorium is dark except for the light used in rehearsal. The Professor is at the piano PLAYING off a new song. Beside him stands Mat, running over the words from a professional copy. Babe, waiting to take charge of the rehearsal, sits under the light glancing over a *Police Gazette*. A cleaning woman is engaged in mopping up. BURLEY ENTERS.

BURLEY

(to cleaning woman)

Is Mr. Norton around?

CLEANING WOMAN

Sure thing. He's in there, sir.

She gestures off. Burley tosses her a silver coin.

BURLEY

Thanks.

CLEANING WOMAN
    Thank *you*, sir.
Burley goes to the gambling room.

INT   GAMBLING ROOM   BURLEY   BLACKIE   CUSTOMER
Burley stops at the door of the gambling room and watches
Blackie at work. Blackie, in his shirt sleeves and wearing an eye
shade, is dealing for one lone customer. The regular dealer is
asleep. Blackie rakes in some winnings.

CUSTOMER
    Well—that lets me out.

BLACKIE
    That all the dough you got?

CUSTOMER
    Every dime.
Blackie slaps down a hundred dollar bill.

> BLACKIE

Here's a hundred bucks, sucker—get yourself a cup of coffee.

> CUSTOMER

Thanks, Blackie.

As Blackie rises,

> BLACKIE

Guess I'd better go to bed.

The CUSTOMER LEAVES. As Blackie turns, he sees Burley. Covering his surprise,

> BLACKIE
> (casually)

Well—good morning, Burley.
> (overly polite)

Anything I can do for you?

> BURLEY

Yes. I want to buy the contract you hold with that girl.

Blackie looks at him a moment, then:

> BLACKIE
> (still casual)

What made you think it was for sale?

> BURLEY
> (in a sarcastically friendly tone)

I don't know why you'd want to be stubborn about it, Norton. You may be needing the money.

> BLACKIE

I'm all right.

> BURLEY

Yes, but you may be in for a few . . . difficulties down here.

Blackie studies him, then:

> BLACKIE

What are you talking about—difficulties?

                        BURLEY
Ever hear of the Johnston Antigambling Ordinance?

                        BLACKIE
Yeah.

                        BURLEY
You're running against the law, you know.

                        BLACKIE
So is every joint in Frisco.

                        BURLEY
                    (with threat)
I'm only telling you—that's all.
Blackie looks at Burley a moment—then:

                        BLACKIE
You seem to have taken quite a "liking" for the little
lady.

                        BURLEY
                    (with sarcasm)
I'm only interested in making her a useful member of
the Tivoli Opera Company!

                        BLACKIE
                    (sarcastically)
Well now, isn't that sweet of you!
As if in defiance, Blackie LAUGHS—then:

                        BLACKIE
I'll tell you what I'll do, Burley. If the little lady *wants* to
leave me, you can have her contract for nothing.
Blackie goes to door leading into auditorium, opens it and looks
o.s.

AUDITORIUM   MARY   BLACKIE   BURLEY
Blackie stands at the open door watching Mary SINGING. We
see Mary singing and Blackie loving it. Burley can be seen in b.g.
behind Blackie. Finally:

                        BLACKIE
                    (calls out commandingly)

Mary!
Mary looks up, sees Blackie and STOPS SINGING.

> BLACKIE (cont'd)
> Come here!

Mary starts for the gambling room.

GAMBLING ROOM   BLACKIE   BURLEY
Blackie turns to Burley and grins confidently—smugly—with braggadocio. Burley smiles but:

> BURLEY
> (with warning)
> You're taking a long chance, Blackie!

> BLACKIE
> (archly, sarcastically)
> Maybe you don't know all *I've got* to offer her!

By which time MARY IS ENTERING the room.

> MARY
> Good morning, Blackie.

Blackie looks her well over.

> BLACKIE
> Good morning.

Burley rises.

> BURLEY
> Good morning, Miss Blake.

Surprised at Burley's presence,

> MARY
> Oh—good morning, Mr. Burley. I want to thank you
> for the lovely roses.

Blackie looks on—criticizing, as usual, Burley's technique with a woman.

> BURLEY
> (to Mary)
> But they were nothing.

BLACKIE
(briskly)
Sit down, kid.

Mary sits.

BLACKIE (cont'd)
Mr. Burley here is trying to buy your contract from me.

Mary looks at Burley.

BURLEY
(to Mary—gallantly)
I told you I wasn't going to give up.

MARY
(thrilled)
You really think I'm ready for the Tivoli?

BURLEY
Yes. And what's more important—Baldini thinks so.

Blackie watches closely.

MARY
(a trace hesitant)
Isn't it my teacher who's talked him into it?

BURLEY
Mme. Albani? Not at all. But the day he heard you singing here convinced him. He believes you can do Marguerite in our first production of *Faust*.

Thrilled to the heart,

MARY
Marguerite!

Blackie's still watching her.

BLACKIE
(cuts in)
What do you say, kid?

Mary faces Blackie—looks at him.

MARY
Would you like to sell my contract, Blackie?

                              BLACKIE
                      (simply)
             No.
A little thrilled in spite of her disappointment, Mary turns to
Burley.

                              MARY
             I'm awfully sorry, Mr. Burley—but you see I can't ac-
             cept.

                              BLACKIE
                      (to Burley—grinning)
             What'd I tell you!
Burley turns to Mary.

                              BURLEY
             But, my dear child—two years in this place may ruin
             your whole career.
She looks at him—says nothing.

                              BLACKIE
                      (cuts in—triumphant—dismissing Burley)
Too bad, Burley. I hope I can do you a favor sometime.
Covering his chagrin, Burley rises and:

                              BURLEY
                      (with sarcasm)
             Thanks, Norton.
Giving up all thought of the Tivoli,

                              MARY
                      (with finality)
             Will you thank Signor Baldini for all his trouble? You've
             both been more than kind.

                              BURLEY
                      (to Mary)
             I'd like to show you another side of San Francisco
             sometime, if I may?

                              MARY
             Thank you.
Burley turns to Blackie.

                    BURLEY
        Good-bye, Norton.
Blackie grins with malice.

                    BLACKIE
        So long.
Burley subtly shows off before Mary by:

                    BURLEY
                (to Blackie)
        You wouldn't like to take five thousand dollars and tear
        up that contract?
Conscious of Burley showing off,

                    BLACKIE
                (amused—contemptuous)
        No.

                    BURLEY
        Ten thousand?

                    BLACKIE
                (simply)
        You trying to make an impression?
Blackie turns to Mary.

                    BLACKIE (cont'd)
                (in casual explanation)
        I told him he could have your contract for nothing if
        you wanted to leave me.
Mary reacts quickly—touched—thrilled. Blackie smiles and
turns to Burley.

                    BLACKIE (cont'd)
        Guess the Tivoli'll have to struggle along, Burley.
Overcome by Blackie's generosity,

                    MARY
        Did you do that, Blackie?

                    BLACKIE
                (still casual)
        Sure.

> (warmly)
> You made your own choice, kid.

Recovering quickly, Burley smiles at Mary and covers his chagrin.

                         BURLEY
       I hope you're never sorry, my dear. Good-bye.

                          MARY
       Good-bye.

BURLEY GOES OUT. Touched to the heart by Blackie's action, Mary turns to him—tears welling into her eyes.

                          MARY
       It was generous of you, Blackie, about my contract!

                         BLACKIE
       Aw—forget it.

Blackie pats her insinuatingly on the shoulder.

                    BLACKIE (cont'd)
       Look, kid. You've heard all about the Tivoli Opera
       House from a lot of mugs that never got around any-
       where. So I'm going to tip you off to a few facts about
       the Paradise. Come on.

He leads her toward his office off the gambling room.

BLACKIE'S OFFICE

BLACKIE leads MARY IN—his arm about her shoulders. There are still traces of tears in Mary's eyes—so touched has she been over the generosity of Blackie's offer to Burley to let her off her contract. As Blackie leads her in,

                         BLACKIE
       Never been in here, have you?

Preoccupied by his sweetness and thrilled by his contact,

                          MARY
       No.

Not noting her mood,

> BLACKIE

Well—I don't do much office work—but here's where I
keep the records.

He leads her to some loving cups.

> BLACKIE (cont'd)

Know what those are?

Mary barely glances at them—then looks back at Blackie.

> MARY

No.

> BLACKIE
> (impressively)

Every year the wine agents in town, Freddy Duane and
the rest of 'em, pull off an event called "The Chickens'
Ball." Ever hear of it?

Mary's mood stays the same. Her gaze never leaving Blackie,
she shakes her head.

> MARY

No.

> BLACKIE

I thought not!

Hitting her on the arm with the back of his hand,

> BLACKIE (cont'd)

Know what happens at that ball?

As she still looks up at him, he PAUSES for effect—then:

> BLACKIE (cont'd)

They hold a competition and give a prize of *ten thousand
dollars in gold* to the proprietor of the joint that puts on
the *most artistic show*. And d'you know the joint that's
won it—*three times running*?

Another slap on her arm with the back of his hand.

> BLACKIE (cont'd)

The Paradise!

Mary's still looking at him—touched—still conscious only of
him.

              MARY
That's . . . that's fine!
In vindication of his place,

             BLACKIE
           (proudly)
And for "artistic achievement." That's what they said in
the speech every time they slipped me the trophy—
"artistic achievement."
Still looking up at him,

             MARY
        (further touched)
Why—it's wonderful!

             BLACKIE
         (warmly)
Well—ain't I telling you!
Blackie CHUCKLES.

         BLACKIE (cont'd)
I'll win it next time, too! And the dough will go for the
campaign fund. For the little mugs down here on the
Coast!
Turning, he looks down at her and sees the expression of love
and admiration in her eyes as she looks at him. There is a moment of SILENCE as they stand thus. Finally, smilingly,

         BLACKIE (cont'd)
        (very softly)
I like to look into those big lamps of yours.
Unable to trust herself, she lowers her eyes. He puts his hand on
her hair—smoothing it.

         BLACKIE (cont'd)
If you ever want to cut any of this, I'll put some in my
watch.
Thrilled—touched—she once more looks up. A PAUSE—then:

         BLACKIE (cont'd)
I'm stuck on you, kid—d'you know it?
Mary, still looking up at him, is unable to speak. Finally with a

sudden movement she turns—goes to the window and looks off—trying to pull herself together. He watches her a moment quizzically—then goes to her.

> BLACKIE
> What's the matter?

She turns further away to hide her feelings.

> BLACKIE (cont'd)
> Turn around here.

He pulls her around—Mary averting her face to keep him from seeing it.

> BLACKIE (cont'd)
> Let's see!

He puts his hand to her chin, forcing her to look up at him. For a moment they stand thus—then:

> BLACKIE (cont'd)
> What is it?

> MARY
> (as if in confession)
> Blackie!

> BLACKIE
> Well, what d'you know—

He LAUGHS.

> BLACKIE (cont'd)
> (relievedly)
> *It's about time!*

Saying which, he gathers her into his arms and kisses her with passion, full on the mouth, Mary relaxing completely, giving in. The kiss over, he looks fondly down on her.

> BLACKIE (cont'd)
> (briskly—proudly)
> Look, kid. I've made a few plans for your future!

He releases her, then proudly goes to his desk, picks up a rolled-up poster and, beaming—with proud satisfaction— proceeds to unroll it.

BLACKIE (cont'd)
Just take a gander at this!
Mary looks at the poster revealing her in tights. The sight of it
stuns, shocks, dazes her. She looks at it aghast. Blackie is too
enthused to note her attitude.

BLACKIE
I've been working on it for weeks! Why—I'll have it on
every billboard in San Francisco.
Blackie admires the poster.

BLACKIE (cont'd)
(almost lovingly)
I wanted it to be a surprise so I got Della Bailey to pose
for the figure. Then they slapped your head on top of
it. Clever art work, eh?
He looks at her. Looking back at him, she recognizes the
thoughtless, boyish enthusiasm which precludes his feeling any
insult in what he has done. Touched by it, in spite of her shock,
but unable to trust herself to words, she nods. Blackie, looking
down at her, puzzled—senses something wrong and is boyishly
hurt. His face falls.

BLACKIE (cont'd)
Don't you like it?
Anguished—tears of disappointment in her eyes, but unable to
hurt him,

MARY
Why, of course.

BLACKIE
(relieved)
Well—I thought so! You'll be *Queen of the Barbary Coast*!
Pinching her cheek,

BLACKIE (cont'd)
For Blackie!
She looks up at him, smiling through her tears.

BLACKIE (cont'd)
Happy?

Still smiling through her tears—smothering her bitter disappointment, she nods. He looks into her eyes a long moment—touched to the depths by her beauty and allure. Finally,

> BLACKIE (cont'd)
> (very softly)
> What d'you say we go up to my place . . . and have some chop suey?

She hesitates.

> BLACKIE (cont'd)
> I'll have Jow Lee cook us up something special.
> (ingratiatingly)
> Come on!

Putting his arm about her shoulder, he leads her out into the auditorium, Mary giving in, realizing what she is headed for, but carried along by his lure. They EXIT slowly—close to each other.

AUDITORIUM   TRIXIE   MAT   OTHERS
Rehearsal is proceeding, Trixie and Mat doing a dance routine. In the auditorium are seated other entertainers. The cleaning woman is still at her task. As BLACKIE leads MARY down through the darkened auditorium, Trixie, looking out, sees him with his arm about Mary and stops cold. Mat's still dancing as:

> MAT
> (to Trixie)
> Whatsa matter, stupid?

He looks off to where Trixie's gaze is centered. Then disgusted—still dancing:

> MAT (cont'd)
> Aw—snap into it!

His arm still about Mary,

> BLACKIE
> (brutally cheerful)
> That's right, Trixie. You can knock off!

They all look at him.

BLACKIE (cont'd)
Everybody's going to drink champagne on me!
The PROFESSOR STOPS PLAYING. They all look at Mary who self-consciously stiffens under their gaze.

BLACKIE (cont'd)
(to Babe)
Dig up some of that Pommery Sec for the boys and girls.
Delighted at Blackie's luck, Babe gazes at Mary and:

BABE
Sure thing!
Babe jumps down and heads for the bar.

BABE (cont'd)
Shall I order you some breakfast, Blackie?

BLACKIE
No, thanks. Mary and I are going upstairs for some chop suey.
They all react—Mat disgusted. Mary stands there self-conscious—fighting within herself—trying hard to gain possession of her will power. The Professor's heartsick for Mary. As he rises,

PROFESSOR
Mary! I have another new number I'd like you to try out.
Mary looks at him—his offer of help giving her a trace more strength.

BLACKIE
(to Professor)
Not *this* morning!
Blackie turns to Mat.

BLACKIE (cont'd)
Mat—go tell Jow Lee—never mind—I'll tell him myself.
Smiling at Mary,

> BLACKIE (cont'd)
>
> Stay right here, honey. I won't be a minute!

She looks at him. He pinches her cheek possessively and turns. She looks at him terrified. BLACKIE EXITS to the kitchen. Mary looks after Blackie—dazed—trying to pull herself out of Blackie's sensuous influence. As she stands there, Mat walks up to her.

> MAT
>
> (sarcastically, as if in congratulation)
>
> Nice going, sister!

He pats her on the shoulder.

> MAT (cont'd)
>
> You've done *all right*!

She looks at him dumbly. He walks OUT OF FRAME. She stands looking off after him—then looks off toward the kitchen where Blackie is. There is a moment more of struggle, but finally her real nature wins out. As if startled, she suddenly turns and rushes headlong OUT of the place, as if running away.

KITCHEN   JOW LEE
The cook, Jow Lee, is fussing about making coffee as BLACKIE ENTERS.

> JOW LEE
>
> Good morning, Boss. You ready for coffee? Make 'em fresh.

> BLACKIE
>
> Look, Jow Lee—I want you to fix up some of that special chop suey for two—the way I like it—with noodles on the side. And bring it upstairs.

> JOW LEE
>
> I got you. Boss very happy this morning.

Grinning, Blackie gives him a little poke.

> BLACKIE
>
> Well—look alive, will you?

> JOW LEE
>
> Sure. Me get a move on.

Jow Lee starts for the cupboard.

                    JOW LEE (cont'd)
          Want to see young lady. Must be nice!
Blackie tosses a silver dollar on the table and goes toward the
auditorium.

AUDITORIUM   CLEANING WOMAN   MAT   OTHERS
As BLACKIE opens the door he bumps into the cleaning woman.

                    BLACKIE
               (happily)
          Knock off there, Maggie.
Blackie kicks over her pail.

                    BLACKIE
          You're going to have champagne.
The cleaning woman jumps up in delight.

                    CLEANING WOMAN
          Me too?
Already heading on his way,

                    BLACKIE
          I'd like to know why not!
Blackie reaches the spot where he left Mary—and he looks up.
Mary is gone. The Professor sits at his piano thoughtful, de-
pressed. Trixie stands leaning dejectedly against the proscenium
arch. In b.g. the others are grouped about a table where Babe is
opening champagne. The CORK POPS LOUDLY—they CHEER
and APPLAUD. Babe pours the champagne. A girl entertainer
holds up her glass of champagne,

                    GIRL ENTERTAINER
               (warmly)
          Here's to Blackie! Bless his heart!
Trixie lets out a BITTER LAUGH, nobody paying her any attention.

                    BLACKIE
          Where's Mary?

MAT

Guess she went up to set the table.

Blackie heads for the front of the auditorium.

BLACKIE

Thanks.

As Blackie barges past the table where the group is drinking, the cleaning woman grabs a glass of champagne.

CLEANING WOMAN
(calls after Blackie)

Here's to you, darlin'! I wish I had me youth!

They LAUGH.

TRIXIE
(bursts out bitterly)

Well—you can have mine.

Stopping for an instant,

BLACKIE
(surprised—as to a child)

Why, Trixie—that's not nice!

LAUGHING, Blackie goes on.

OTHERS
(quieting her)

Sure, Trixie—pipe down!

Don't be that way, Trixie!

Here, have a drink!

Trixie stands staring straight ahead. To counteract Trixie's contretemps, Babe holds up his glass.

BABE
(calls after Blackie)

Tell Mary *here's to 'er*!

Mat holds up his glass.

MAT
(facetiously)

Sure! Everyone to his own taste as the old woman said when she kissed the cow!

He ROARS—the others all LAUGH. Blackie is now at the door.

                    BLACKIE
           (calls back to Babe, happily)
     When that runs out, Babe—open up some more!

                    BABE
        You bet!
BLACKIE GOES OUT.

EXT   PARADISE   BLACKIE
Blackie comes out to the street where he turns and hurries to the
door leading up to his apartment.

                    TIM (OS)
        Blackie!
Blackie looks down. TIM is heading for Blackie.

                    BLACKIE
           (a trace impatient)
        Hello, Tim.

                    TIM
     I came over to talk about your campaign, kid.

                    BLACKIE
     Oh, fine, Tim. But could we make it a little later?

                    TIM
        Sure!
Blackie turns.

                    TIM (cont'd)
        Oh, by the way, Blackie, I just saw Mary.
Blackie stops.

                    BLACKIE
        You did?
Tim looks at him squarely.

                    TIM
        I put her in a cab just now.
Blackie looks at him—just looks.

TIM (cont'd)
She said to tell you good-bye—and that she's taking you up on your offer to let her off that contract.

BLACKIE
(aghast)
What's that?

TIM
Didn't you say she could go?

BLACKIE
Yes. But—

TIM
Well, she's gone to the Tivoli.
Blackie looks at him. Tim puts his hand on Blackie's shoulder.

TIM (cont'd)
I'm glad you did it, Blackie! This was no place for her.
Beginning to burn,

BLACKIE
You think not, eh?

TIM
Of course not! And you knew it!
Looking him right in the eye,

TIM (cont'd)
Didn't you?

BLACKIE
(with just a shade of resentment)
D'you think she'd be better off at the Tivoli—*in the hands of Jack Burley?*

TIM
(smiling)
She'll be *safe* with Burley, Blackie. She doesn't *love him*!
Blackie looks right at him a moment, then LAUGHS ironically.

BLACKIE

You like chop suey, Tim, don't you?

TIM
(mystified)

Sure.

Enjoying the "joke" on himself—yet burning underneath,

BLACKIE

Well, come on upstairs! We're going to have some.

As he starts on up, Tim following—

FADE OUT.

FADE IN:

EXT   CLOSE SHOT   TIVOLI OPERA HOUSE   SIGN   NIGHT
An electric sign reads: "Tivoli Opera House." The CAMERA PULLS BACK revealing the old Tivoli. There is a great stir of PEOPLE arriving for the opera. There are all sorts—most of them in evening dress. Smart carriages are driving up, etc., etc.

DISSOLVE TO:

INT   MARY'S DRESSING ROOM   MARY   LOUISE   ALBANI
Mary's dressing room is filled with flowers. Mary, nervous, hectic, excited, is putting the last touches to her make-up as Marguerite. However, over her excitement there is a shadow of preoccupation. She is thinking of Blackie. Mary's maid, LOUISE, stands in attendance and her teacher, MME. ALBANI, a big motherly Italian, is sitting nearby. O.s. SOUNDS of MUSICIANS TUNING UP.

ALBANI

Relax, my child, relax! There's no reason to worry! Why—when you can sing to please Albani—

She gestures toward herself with her thumb.

ALBANI (cont'd)

—the rest of it is easy!

A KNOCK ON DOOR—the maid goes to open it. Mary affectionately pinches Albani's cheek.

MARY

I'm afraid you're prejudiced!

The maid opens the door on BURLEY.

> BURLEY
> Good evening, ladies.

> ALBANI
> (kiddingly)
> Good evening and get out! This child has a perform-
> ance to give.

As she smiles at Albani,

> MARY
> Let him come in, Albani.

Mary gestures toward the flowers.

> MARY (cont'd)
> He has to be thanked for all this.

> ALBANI
> (kiddingly suspicious)
> *Alone*, I suppose.

Burley LAUGHS.

> BURLEY
> That's right.

> ALBANI
> (to maid)
> Get out, Louisa!

Giving the maid a little spank she ushers her OUT of the room.

> ALBANI (cont'd)
> (to Burley)
> In *my* day—the Opera came *first*!

Saying which she GOES OUT, closing the door. Burley
LAUGHS—then—

> BURLEY
> (heartily—warmly—giving it great
> importance)
> My mother's out there tonight, Mary.

> MARY
> She is?

> BURLEY

Yes . . . she came all the way back from New York.
Guess she was tired of reading about you in my letters.

Mary looks at him—a little surprised. Burley briskly takes her
two hands.

> BURLEY (cont'd)

In another two hours you'll be famous, but before
you've got the whole town at your feet I want to put in
my bid. I love you, dear! I want to marry you!

Mary looks at him in utter surprise.

> BURLEY (cont'd)

What is it?

> MARY

Why—

> BURLEY

I've always wanted you—from the first moment I set
eyes on you, but I didn't realize then how I wanted
you.

Mary looks at him, touched but anguished—hesitant.

> BURLEY (cont'd)

Don't try to answer me now. I just wanted to let you
know how I felt. Good luck, dear!

Saying which he kisses her hands—drops them and heads for
the door. As he goes, Mary stands stock still, looking straight
ahead—thinking of Blackie, anguish on her face and tears welling up in her eyes.

HALL OUTSIDE DRESSING ROOM   BURLEY

Burley goes right on out of the dressing room and closes the
door. He heads for entrance to front of the house. O.s. TUNING
UP OF MUSICIANS becomes more hectic. As Burley goes, various BACK-STAGE TYPES greet him with great respect. A singer
in costume:

> SINGER

Good evening, Mr. Burley.

BURLEY

Good evening.

STAGE MANAGER

Good evening, Mr. Burley.

BURLEY

Good evening, Jim.

As he reaches the door leading out front—a stage hand opens it.

BURLEY

(to stage hand)

Thanks.

STAGE HAND

Not at all, Mr. Burley.

By which time Burley is through the door. It closes—Burley turns and parts the curtains of a stage box.

STAGE BOX   MRS. BURLEY   SOCIETY WOMAN   DUANE

Burley's mother, MRS. BURLEY, a hearty old lady of seventy, exquisitely dressed and covered with jewels, is seated with another society woman and Freddy Duane. Mrs. Burley looks up as BURLEY ENTERS the doorway.

BURLEY

I'll be right with you, darling. I want to take a look out front.

Mrs. Burley, smiling, kisses her hand to her son who returns the caress and then heads for the front of the house.

CORRIDOR   BURLEY   OTHERS

As Burley goes through the corridor, people heading for other boxes greet him. O.s. the OVERTURE STARTS.

YOUNG WOMAN

Hello, Jack.

BURLEY

(heartily)

Good evening, Beth.

OLD LADY

Good evening, Mr. Burley. What a thrilling first night!

               BURLEY
Yes—isn't it.
By which time he nears the HEAD USHER.

               BURLEY (cont'd)
              (to Head Usher)
Have you seen Signor Baldini?

               HEAD USHER
Not yet, sir.
Burley goes on out into the lobby.

LOBBY   BURLEY   OTHERS
Burley comes through the crowded lobby, passing by a line of
people entering the theatre.

             PROMINENT-LOOKING MAN
Hello, Jack! Big night, eh?

               BURLEY
You bet it is, Senator!
At which point he sees BLACKIE, followed by BABE, both in
white tie and tails, heading in from the street. Surprised, Burley
stops.

               BURLEY
             (overly effusive)
Well—good evening, Norton!
Burley nods to Babe.

               BLACKIE
             (pleasantly)
Good evening.

               BABE
          (in unison, grinning)
Evening.

               BURLEY
             (gloatingly)
I didn't know you were a first nighter!
Going right on his way,

BLACKIE
(unconcernedly)
I am tonight. I came to close you up.

BURLEY
(in amused surprise)
Just a moment.
Blackie stops—he LAUGHS.

BURLEY (cont'd)
What did you say?

BLACKIE
To close you up. You've got a girl appearing here that's
under contract to me.
Blackie starts away again.

BURLEY
(still as if amused)
Oh, no, I haven't.
Blackie stops—Burley smiling.

BURLEY (cont'd)
You abrogated that contract, Norton—gave her per-
mission to leave.

BLACKIE
Sure. I gave her her choice and she *said* she'd stay with
me. So the contract stands.
Turning, Blackie gestures off.

BLACKIE (cont'd)
See that man over there—the one with the big black
mustache?
Burley looks over and sees a PROCESS SERVER, a big mean-look-
ing mug, standing in the lobby eating peanuts from a bag. The
Process Server looks over toward Blackie—very smug and salutes. As he answers the man's salute,

BLACKIE
(to Burley)
That big, stupid man represents the law. And he's got a

paper in his pocket that's going to stop your prima
donna right in the middle of her first cantata. Now isn't
that just awful?
Burley is now really alarmed, but with overassurance, LAUGH-
ING, he puts up a front.

> BURLEY
> You wouldn't do that, Norton.

> BLACKIE
> (sarcastically sorry)
> Sorry, Burley, but I thoughtlessly started the man go-
> ing. And I couldn't do a thing with him now.

O.s. we hear the MUSIC OF THE OPERA.

> BLACKIE (cont'd)
> Well—I guess I'll go and get my star.

Blackie starts in. Covering his concern, Burley tries to anxiously
stall for time.

> BURLEY
> She doesn't go on till the second act, Norton.

Blackie stops.

> BLACKIE
> That's not very good showmanship.

Burley smiles.

> BLACKIE (cont'd)
> (to Babe)
> We'll wait. I don't want to listen to those other mugs.

> BURLEY
> (smilingly—gracious)
> Won't you smoke a cigar while you're waiting?

Burley fumbles in his pocket. Blackie takes out a fancy cigar
lighter. Burley fumbles in his pocket a moment longer—then:

> BURLEY
> I'll get one.

Saying which he heads for the office of the theatre. As he passes
an elegant lady,

ELEGANT LADY

Good evening, Mr. Burley! We can't wait to hear the new star!

BURLEY
(quizzically)
Thanks.

Near the entrance to the office he passes BALDINI who stands rubbing his hands in satisfaction over the big opening.

BURLEY
(to Baldini, grimly)
Come in here!

Surprised at Burley's tone,

BALDINI

What is it?

BURLEY

Come on!

Burley drags him into the office.

OFFICE   BURLEY   BALDINI

The office is empty as Burley and Baldini come in. Burley shuts the door—so the MUSIC is NO LONGER HEARD. Baldini is further surprised.

BALDINI

What is it?

Without answering, Burley goes to the phone.

BURLEY

Hello. Hello, Central? Get me Fillmore 2871.

Burley turns to Baldini—breaking into a cold sweat.

BURLEY (cont'd)
Norton's got a Sheriff here to stop Mary Blake.

BALDINI
(aghast)
Stop her?

                    BURLEY
           Yes! During the performance!

                    BALDINI
                   (aghast)
           But he can't do that!

                    BURLEY
                  (in phone)
           Hello. Is Mr. Davis there?
Burley turns to Baldini.

                 BURLEY (cont'd)
           Maybe he can!
Baldini is goggle-eyed.

                 BURLEY (cont'd)
                  (in phone)
           Hello. Davis? This is Jack Burley. I want you to hurry
           right over to the Tivoli Opera House with a restraining
           order—to hold up a process.
There's a pause—o.s. an INDISTINGUISHABLE MUMBLE comes
over the phone.

                 BURLEY (cont'd)
           What's that?
A pause—o.s. the MUMBLE. Then:

                 BURLEY (cont'd)
                  (angrily)
           I don't care if the office closed ten hours ago. *Find him!*
O.s. another MUMBLE.

                 BURLEY (cont'd)
           But I've *got* to have it!
As o.s. MUMBLE becomes very apologetic in tone, Burley SLAMS
up the receiver.

                    BALDINI
                   (aghast)
           What is it?
As he heads for the lobby,

BURLEY
You'd better get backstage. I'll see what I can do.
Pulling himself together Burley reassumes his air of amused nonchalance. He opens the door and GOES OUT.

LOBBY   BURLEY   BLACKIE   BABE   PROCESS SERVER
Burley goes out to where Blackie stands backed up by Babe and the Process Server. Burley reaches into the pocket in which he fumbled unsuccessfully before and now pulls out an elegant cigar case filled with cigars.

BURLEY
(very gracious and nonchalant)
Here you are, Norton.

BLACKIE
Thanks.
Blackie takes a cigar. Burley hands the case to Babe who grins and takes one. Blackie reads the name of the cigar band questioningly.

BLACKIE (cont'd)
Cameo, eh?

BURLEY
(a touch razzingly)
Didn't think you'd know *that* brand down at the Paradise.

BLACKIE
That's right.
Blackie lights the cigar.

BLACKIE (cont'd)
You needn't have bothered to call up Davis, Burley. I could have told you that deputy of his was off on a deep sea fishing trip. He's crazy about fishing so I chartered him a boat.
Burley looks at him a moment—smiles—then dropping his pose of nonchalance becomes businesslike.

BURLEY

What about a deal, Norton? I'll give you fifteen thousand dollars for that contract.

BLACKIE

(sarcastically overgracious)

I'd like to oblige you, Burley, but you see it's out of my hands.

Blackie gestures to the Process Server who is standing right beside them.

BLACKIE (cont'd)

And this Process Server is the meanest man west of the Rocky Mountains! He'd push his mother off a ferry boat for half a dollar. He'd turn off the air in a baby's incubator just to watch the little sucker squirm.

The Process Server, taking no notice at all of Blackie's remarks, goes right on munching peanuts.

BLACKIE (cont'd)

(to Process Server)

Well, Jim—what do you say?

PROCESS SERVER

The quicker I stop her, the quicker I get home.

Blackie holds out the cigar.

BLACKIE

(to Babe)

See that we never order any of these for the Paradise.

Saying which he tosses the cigar away. Burley reacts—Babe grins and throws his cigar after Blackie's—they go on in.

THEATRE AISLE   BLACKIE   BABE   HEAD USHER   PROCESS SERVER

Blackie gives the tickets to the Head Usher who leads them down to the stage box. O.s. the MUSIC is that just preceding the "Jewel Song."

STAGE BOX

The USHER opens the curtains and shows in BLACKIE, BABE and the PROCESS SERVER. As Blackie heads for front of box,

STAGE
Mary is making her entrance for the "Jewel Song."

CLOSE SHOT   STAGE BOX   BLACKIE
Blackie, still standing, looks at Mary—smug—grinning.

CLOSE SHOT   STAGE   MARY
Mary, looking off, sees Blackie. For just a moment she wavers, and then pulling herself together, she begins to SING.

STAGE BOX   BLACKIE   BABE   PROCESS SERVER
Blackie sits—looks at stage—then looks at the big ORCHESTRA, then around at the brilliant-looking AUDIENCE and, obviously impressed by it all, begins thoughtfully to rub his chin.

                    PROCESS SERVER
          Shall I go back now?

                    BLACKIE
          No. I'll tell you when.
The Process Server, impatient, stands at back of box near the door.

BACK OF THEATRE   BURLEY
Burley stands at the back of the theatre—looking at Blackie and the Process Server—watches narrowly.

STAGE   MARY
Mary, conscious of Blackie's presence, SINGS as if singing to him.

BACK OF THEATRE   BURLEY
Burley looks at Mary—half realizing her feelings toward Blackie—worried—concerned.

CLOSE SHOT   STAGE   MARY
Mary is SINGING through a beautiful and tuneful passage.

STAGE BOX   BLACKIE   BABE   PROCESS SERVER
The Process Server is impatient and fidgeting.

                    BABE
              (sotto voce)
          Say, Blackie, that's kinda pretty.

Beginning to be moved by her singing, yet not wanting to admit much,

                    BLACKIE
     Yeah.

ORCHESTRA   TIM
Tim is seated in the orchestra—listening—thrilled.

GALLERY   PROFESSOR
The Professor—in the gallery—is watching Mary tensely.

STAGE BOX   BLACKIE
Blackie—listening, thoughtfully moved—touched.

ORCHESTRA   TIM
Tim, pleased over Blackie's attitude, looks back at stage.

CLOSE SHOT   STAGE   MARY
Mary—SINGING to the end of the "Jewel Song"—inspired—ending brilliantly.

AUDIENCE
The audience APPLAUDS LOUDLY and with enthusiasm.

STAGE BOX   BLACKIE   BABE   PROCESS SERVER
Babe and Blackie look out over the AUDIENCE, Blackie thoughtful, moved in spite of himself. The Process Server starts to rise.

                    BLACKIE
     Sit down.

                    PROCESS SERVER
          (sore)
     Say, what's the idea?—I didn't come to this opera to
     hear the opera!

                    BLACKIE
     Sit down!
The Process Server begins to burn.

CLOSE SHOT   BACK OF THEATRE   BURLEY
Burley is watching Blackie closely, wonderingly.

CLOSE SHOT   STAGE   MARY
Mary acknowledges the APPLAUSE—then starts again to SING.
                                        DISSOLVE TO:

MONTAGE   OPERA SCENES   MARY   BLACKIE
We see several of the most tuneful numbers from *Faust* in a
SERIES OF QUICK VORKAPICH SHOTS interspersed with CLOSE
SHOTS of MARY as she SINGS and BLACKIE as he listens. Blackie
is increasingly moved by the beauty of the music and of Mary's
singing. The LAST SCENE OF THE MONTAGE is Mary and the
tenor toward the end of a duet—they sing through to the finish.

AUDIENCE
The audience, warmly enthusiastic, APPLAUDS.

STAGE BOX   BLACKIE   BABE   PROCESS SERVER
The Process Server looks bored and very sore. The CAMERA
MOVES to include just Blackie and Babe.

                     BABE
        Gee, Blackie, I think she's great!
More moved than he likes to admit,

                    BLACKIE
        Not bad.

                     BABE
        Kinda seems too bad to choke her off.
Babe turns to look at the Process Server—his mouth opens wide
in amazement. Blackie's gaze follows Babe's. THE CAMERA
PULLS BACK revealing that the Process Server's chair is empty.

                     BABE
        He's gone on back!
Blackie thinks a second—then, his face set—rises, rushes out of
the box toward backstage.

STAGE AND WINGS
On stage the opera is proceeding with the MUSIC which follows
the duet. Just as the PROCESS SERVER reaches the wings,
BLACKIE pounces on him, grabbing him by the coat collar and

whirling him around. Two nearby STAGE HANDS look up, surprised. Blackie hauls off, knocks the Process Server cold with one slug. The stage hands move up apprehensively.

                         BLACKIE
                 (to stage hands, sotto voce)
            It's all right, boys.
Blackie kneels by the Process Server.

                    BLACKIE (cont'd)
            Nothin' to worry about.
Saying which, he takes the summons from the unconscious man's pocket and puts it in his own for safe-keeping.
                                         DISSOLVE TO:

LONG SHOT   STAGE
The magnificent third act FINALE with Faust, Marguerite and Mephistopheles begins.

BACK OF THEATER   BURLEY
Burley looks on, relieved that nothing has happened, and wipes his forehead.

MRS. BURLEY'S BOX   MRS. BURLEY
Mrs. Burley looks delightedly at Mary.

GALLERY   PROFESSOR
The Professor is entranced.

ORCHESTRA   TIM
Tim watches in rapture.

STAGE BOX   BLACKIE   BABE
Blackie and Babe watch and listen intently.

STAGE
The trio SINGS through to a magnificent end.

AUDIENCE
The audience rising, goes mad in APPLAUSE.

ORCHESTRA   TIM
Tim, tears in his eyes, APPLAUDING wildly. O.s. through the

APPLAUSE the ORCHESTRA continues to the end of the act—which is only a few bars.

GALLERY   PROFESSOR
He's APPLAUDING wildly.

STAGE
The curtain is down. The trio, including MARY, comes out and acknowledge the APPLAUSE. Mary ventures a glance toward Blackie.

STAGE BOX   BLACKIE   MARY'S POV
Blackie, standing in the box, gets Mary's look and swelling up, straightens his tie.

STAGE AND WINGS   TRIO INCLUDING MARY
From backstage we see the trio making its last bow—the curtain comes down. The tenor and bass escort Mary offstage. Waiting in the wings is MME. ALBANI. She enfolds Mary in her arms and bursts into a rigmarole of Italian endearments—keeping one arm about her protectingly. BURLEY rushes up.

> BURLEY
> Mary! You've made history tonight! History!

Others start to gather around.

> MARY
> Oh thanks! Thanks!

She begins to glance about, hoping to see Blackie. BALDINI rushes up to Mary.

> BALDINI
> My child! You were superb!

He kisses her on both cheeks.

> BALDINI (cont'd)
> (to Albani)
> She is *made*, Marcellina!

> ALBANI
> (proudly)
> What did I tell you!

Baldini kisses Albani. Burley gestures to STANDING, a news-
paperman.

BURLEY
(to Mary)
This is Mr. Standing of the *Examiner*! He says you are
greater than Nielson!

MARY
Oh thank you, Mr. Standing!

STANDING
You have a great future, Miss Blake!
The PROFESSOR breaks through the ever-gathering crowd.

PROFESSOR
Wunderbar! Sie haben kolossal gesungen!
Wringing the Professor's hand,

MARY
(warmly)
Professor!
He kisses her hand.

ALBANI
Leave her alone now! Come, child. Come on!
She leads her off through the crowd. A YOUNG WOMAN crowds
up to Mary.

YOUNG WOMAN
May I have a photograph?

ALBANI
Look out everybody. Don't crowd!
They continue on toward the dressing room.

YOUNG MAN REPORTER
May I have an interview for the *Dramatic Review*?
Still looking about for Blackie,

MARY
Yes, tomorrow.
They reach the dressing room door. Albani opens it and ushers
Mary in.

DRESSING ROOM
It is filled with flowers. MARY and ALBANI ENTER, look up and see Blackie. He is standing beside the dressing table looking down on a stack of cards which have been removed from the flowers. He looks up. Frantic with relief at seeing him,

                    MARY
          Blackie!

                    BLACKIE
               (a little embarrassed)
          Hello, kid.
Mary looks at him a moment longer—then:

                    MARY
               (to Albani)
          Mme. Albani, I—
ALBANI understandingly goes on OUT—closing the door. Mary turns and looks toward Blackie. As he picks up the top card,

                    BLACKIE
          Looks like Burley's getting a little careless—putting things down on paper.

                    MARY
               (simply)
          He's asked me to marry him.

                    BLACKIE
               (amazed)
          No! On the level?
LAUGHING—he tosses the card contemptuously back on the table—then—turning—looks at Mary who stands looking at him. He takes her all in—then:

                    BLACKIE (cont'd)
          You were all right tonight, kid.

                    MARY
               (eagerly)
          Did you think so, Blackie? Really?

> BLACKIE
>
> Say—I'm not going to hold out against those three thousand mugs that went nuts over you.

As she looks up at him thrilled—her eyes shining—he PAUSES a moment—then:

> BLACKIE (cont'd)
> (thoughtfully)
> I haven't caught this opera racket up to now. How long's it been going on?

> MARY
> (smiling)
> About a hundred and fifty years.

> BLACKIE
> (amazed)
> No foolin'?

Mary nods. Condescendingly giving it his approval,

> BLACKIE (cont'd)
> Well, it's all right!

Blackie looks down into her face, taking her all in. A long PAUSE as she looks up at him.

> BLACKIE (cont'd)
> (finally)
> D'you know I'm proud of you?

> MARY
> Is that all . . . Blackie?

> BLACKIE
> All?

> MARY
> (softly)
> Do you love me?

> BLACKIE
> Sure!

A happy PAUSE—then:

MARY

You haven't said so.

BLACKIE

Aw—I love you, kid.
Blackie LAUGHS—then:

BLACKIE (cont'd)

I never sprung that line but once—twenty-five years ago.

MARY

Who was she?

BLACKIE

Just a kid I knew. I haven't seen her lately—she's up in San Quentin.

MARY

And I'm the second, eh?

BLACKIE

Aw—you're the *first!*
Saying which, he gathers her into his arms and kisses her with passion. The kiss over, Mary rests in his arms a moment in complete bliss and SILENCE—then:

MARY

(softly)

Will you marry me, Blackie?
There's a moment's PAUSE while Blackie's brain tries to assimilate this strange new thought. Blackie looks at her, then finally:

BLACKIE

Marry you?

MARY

(softly)

Yes.
There is another long PAUSE. Blackie thinks—Mary looking eagerly up into his face. Blackie dropping his hold on her steps back—looks her up and down—then smiling:

BLACKIE
(in a fondly kidding tone)
I'm a sucker if you aren't the most *domestic* woman—
Mary looks anguished, her chin quivers. She turns away. Blackie pinches her cheek.

BLACKIE (cont'd)
But if that's the only thing in the world that would
make you happy—
Blackie LAUGHS.

BLACKIE (cont'd)
—the gang always said I'd wind up a sucker.
He takes her in his arms.

MARY
Blackie!
Ecstatically she throws her arms about his neck. O.s. there's a
KNOCK ON THE DOOR. A PAUSE—then pulling herself to-
gether:

MARY
(calls)
Come in.
The door is opened by TIM who comes right in.

TIM
Mary!
Seeing Blackie, his face lights up.

TIM (cont'd)
Blackie! How are you, boy?

BLACKIE
(smugly)
Feeling pretty sharp!

TIM
You were great, Mary! I had to fight my way through
half of Frisco to get back here!
Unable to withhold the news,

MARY
Father Tim! Blackie and I—we're going to be married!
A look of triumphant relief comes over Tim's face. He looks over
Mary's shoulder toward Blackie.

BLACKIE
That's right, Tim. The little girl's harpooned me.
Saying which, he glances into a full-length mirror and fixes his
tie. Tim LAUGHS at Blackie, then:

TIM
(to Mary, from his heart)
Guess you know how I feel about it, Mary!
Taking Mary's hands—squeezes them—then, going to Blackie:

TIM
(kiddingly, fondly)
So she "harpooned" you, eh? The girl any man in
Frisco would give his right arm for—and she's "harpooned" you!

Blackie grins disarmingly. Patting Blackie on the shoulder,

> TIM (cont'd)
> (warmly, seriously)
> I'm not going to *wish* you the best of everything in the world, Blackie—'cause you've got it already!

> BLACKIE

Thanks, Tim.
Tim PAUSES—he looks at them.

> TIM

> Well—I know you two would like me to stay—but I'm afraid I've got to be running along.
Tim goes to the door—turns.

> TIM (cont'd)
> Of course, if you insist—

> BLACKIE

Twenty-three! Skidoo!
Blackie makes a pass at Tim who ducks, opens the door and bumps right into BURLEY.

> TIM
> I beg your pardon, Mr. Burley.

> BURLEY

Good evening, Father.
TIM GOES OUT. As Burley enters,

> BURLEY
> (to Mary)
> Why—you haven't changed yet.
At which point he sees Blackie. A PAUSE as they look at each other—then:

> BURLEY (cont'd)
> (challengingly)
> Well—Norton?
Blackie swells up.

BLACKIE

I just came back to congratulate my fiancée!
Burley looks at him utterly aghast—then turns to Mary.

MARY
(heartsick for him)

I'm sorry, Jack!
There is another PAUSE as Burley looks at her, too stunned to
speak.

BLACKIE
(briskly)

Better get out of that rig, babe. The gang's waiting to
celebrate your home-coming.

MARY
(a trace surprised)

Where?

BLACKIE

Down home—at the Paradise. They're waiting for you
to sing "San Francisco!"

MARY

The Paradise?

BURLEY

You don't mean you want to make her go back there
now, Norton?

BLACKIE

What kind of a chump do you take me for? I'm going to
marry her, ain't I?
Blackie turns to Mary, sees the look of anguish on her face . . .
utterly surprised.

BLACKIE (cont'd)

Well—what d'you *want*, kid—me—or this?
There is a long PAUSE as it sinks into her consciousness what
she is being asked to give up. Both men watch her. Dazedly she
looks around the room—thinking.

FADE OUT.

FADE IN:

EXT   CLOSE SHOT   PARADISE   THE POSTER
Posted on the street front of the Paradise is the poster of Mary in tights. A printed streamer across it reads:
      Opening tonight—late star of the Tivoli Opera Co.
O.s. the HOT MUSIC of the Paradise is heard. CAMERA PULLING BACK reveals the street front of the Paradise at the zenith of its night activity. People are crowding in—many of them swells in evening clothes. In b.g. BABE stands in the doorway beaming over the big business. TIM ENTERS THE SCENE, heading straight into the Paradise—on his face an expression of outraged determination. As he passes the poster, TWO SAILORS also pass it. The FIRST SAILOR leers at the poster.

                    FIRST SAILOR
      Some baby!

                    SECOND SAILOR
            (to poster)
      Oh you chicken!

                    BABE (OS)
      Good evening, Father.
Tim looks up as BABE COMES INTO THE SHOT.

                    TIM
      Good evening.

                    BABE
      Great business tonight.

                    TIM
            (grimly)
      Tell Mr. Norton I want to see him.

                    BABE
      Sure thing.
BABE ENTERS the Paradise.

INT   PARADISE   AUDITORIUM   BABE
Babe makes his way through the NOISY auditorium. On the

stage a big chorus number—the theatre crowded. BABE passes
to backstage.

BACKSTAGE   BABE
Backstage Babe runs into MAT made up for his number.

> BABE
>
> Is Blackie back here?

> MAT
> (laconically)
>
> Yeah.

> BABE
>
> Where?

> MAT
> (with disgust)
>
> Where'd you think?

Babe heads for dressing room door, and KNOCKS.

> MARY (OS)
>
> Come in.

Babe opens door and goes in.

DRESSING ROOM   MARY   BLACKIE   BABE
It is garishly decorated with posters—one of them the poster of
Mary, and another an election poster of Blackie. Mary, dressed
in the garish outfit of tights pictured in the poster, is seated at
the makeup shelf arranging her makeup, her manner one of
game determination to go through with what is ahead of her.
With it all she is happy. Blackie stands beside her, leaning
against the shelf. Stunned by his first look at Mary's costume,

> BABE
>
> Gee!
> (to Blackie)
> Looks pretty sharp, eh?

> BLACKIE
> (patronizingly)
>
> She's all right!

Still looking Mary over,

BABE

Father Mullin's out there, Blackie—wants to see you.

Mary, uncomfortable, pulls around the long cape which hangs
from her shoulders so as to cover herself. Watching Mary,

BLACKIE

(to Babe)

Well, bring him back.

Babe casts one last admiring look at Mary and goes OUT closing
the door.

BLACKIE (cont'd)

(to Mary)

You're a funny kid.

Mary looks at him questioningly. Blackie indicates the cape
pulled about her.

BLACKIE (cont'd)

The way you act anyone'd think that wasn't becoming.

She smiles wanly. Blackie goes to her—caresses her hair.

BLACKIE (cont'd)

Happy?

MARY

Yes.

She rises—turns—looks at him—then, as if trying to convince
herself:

MARY (cont'd)

I'm happy!

BLACKIE

That's right!

He takes her in his arms, holds her. Mary smiles—looking into
his face:

MARY

Blackie—let's set the date for our wedding. So we can
tell Father Tim, eh?

BLACKIE

(evasively)

Well sure—anytime . . . of course, it's got to be after election.

Mary tries to hide her disappointment.

> MARY

Has it?

> BLACKIE

Sure. The mob down here knows how I've always kidded that sort of thing.

Blackie LAUGHS.

> BLACKIE (cont'd)

I can't back down and make a fool of myself before election—it'd lose me too many votes.

> MARY
> (her heart sinking)

I see.

> BLACKIE
> (seriously)

It means a lot to me, honey, to win this fight. Not just to put it over on Burley—
> (warmly)
—but *for the Coast*! Understand?

Touched by him she nods.

> BLACKIE (cont'd)

But the first chance I get we'll sneak off to Sacramento and I'll let you slip that halter on me.

He kisses her lightly on the forehead.

> BLACKIE (cont'd)
> (fondly)

Never thought I'd be so nuts about *anyone*!

She smiles up at him. O.s. a KNOCK ON DOOR.

> BLACKIE

Come in.

TIM opens the door and enters.

BLACKIE
(very glib)
Hello, Tim.

Pulling her cape further about her,

MARY
Good evening, Father.

They both note the expression of outrage on his face.

BLACKIE
What's wrong?

TIM
Have you gone out of your mind?

BLACKIE
(innocently)
Why?

TIM
Showing Mary—like this—to that mob out there!

BLACKIE
"Like this?" What's wrong with her?

TIM
Wrong!

BLACKIE
Sure. What's wrong with me being proud to show her off?

Putting up a terrific effort to make Blackie realize what he's doing,

TIM
Blackie, don't you understand what I'm trying to tell you!

BLACKIE
But look, Tim! I'm making her Queen of the Coast! See that poster! Five thousand of 'em will be plastered all over Frisco tomorrow! And ten thousand little ones— for ash cans and the front of trolley cars.

TIM
I'm not going to let you do this, Blackie.
Beginning to get sore,

BLACKIE
I don't get you, Tim. You never butted in on me before.

TIM
Well, I am now! You're not going to exploit this girl!

BLACKIE
Come here, Mary!
Mary joins Blackie. He puts his arm about her shoulder.

BLACKIE (cont'd)
Will you please tell his "holiness" you made up your
own mind to come back?
As if hypnotized,

MARY
I love him, Father.

TIM
That isn't *love*, Mary.
Beginning to rapidly lose control,

BLACKIE
Is that so? Well—it happens to suit *me*!

TIM
It isn't love—to let him drag you down to his level!

BLACKIE
Wait a minute, Tim! *I'm going to marry her!*

TIM
Not if I can stop you!
Blackie looks at him utterly aghast.

TIM (cont'd)
You can't take a woman in marriage and then sell her
immortal soul!

BLACKIE
(utterly contemptuous)
"Immortal soul!"
Blackie LAUGHS razzingly.

BLACKIE (cont'd)
I don't go for that kind of talk, Tim! Don't believe that
nonsense and never have! You'd better get back to the
half-wits that do.
Tim, shocked, reacts. Mary is still dazed, expressionless. O.s. A
KNOCK ON DOOR and:

STAGE MANAGER (OS)
Mary's on next!
Tim takes Mary's long cape from the hook on the wall.*

TIM
Come on, Mary. Come with me.
At the end of his control,

BLACKIE
Wait a moment. I'm running this place! You take care of
your suckers—I'll take care of mine!
Mary stands expressionless.

TIM
She's not going out there!

BLACKIE
(warningly)
I've stood for this psalm-singing blather of yours for
years and never squawked. But you can't drag it in
here! This is *my* joint!
O.s. MUSIC starts up introduction to "San Francisco" and
there's another KNOCK ON DOOR.

STAGE MANAGER (OS)
Mary! Mary Blake!
Tim moves over and takes his stand in front of the door, block-
ing Mary's way.

*Mary was wearing the cape when Tim entered and did not remove it.
—Ed.

TIM
(firmly—quietly)
She's not going out there!
Blackie looks at him one brief moment—then hauls off and socks
Tim squarely on the jaw. Tim stands there—taking it and making no move to defend himself. Blood starts to trickle from his
mouth. Mary watches, still expressionless. O.s. the ORCHESTRA
repeats the introduction to "San Francisco."

STAGE MANAGER (OS)
They're playing Mary's introduction!

BLACKIE
(to Mary)
Get out there, kid!

MARY
I'm not going, Blackie!
He turns and looks at her—she takes off her headdress.

MARY (cont'd)
I'm going with Father Mullin.
Blackie is livid—white.

BLACKIE
If you leave now, you're never coming back!
As answer she takes cape from Tim and puts it on. TIM leads
MARY OUT, leaving the door open. As Blackie stands looking
after them in a white fury, from o.s. come the SOUNDS of fur-
niture being smashed and glass crashing. MAT appears in the
door—frightened—white—excited:

MAT
It's Burley, Blackie! He's giving us the works!
Still Blackie stands livid, looking off after Mary and Tim.

MAT (cont'd)
(shouting)
I coulda told you you couldn't buck his dough and the
influence he's—
Still looking off livid,

                                BLACKIE
                   (cutting in)
      Shut up!
Amazed at his attitude, Mat grabs Blackie by the arm.

                               MAT
    Come on out and get a gander!
BLACKIE FOLLOWS MAT OUT.

BACKSTAGE   MAT   BLACKIE   OTHERS
In b.g. through stage door which is being held open by some gaping actors, we see the gambling room where POLICEMEN are SMASHING up the wheels, etc., etc., creating utter destruction. O.s. the ORCHESTRA continues to play "San Francisco." Blackie takes one brief glance at the destruction—then turns and once more looks after Mary and Tim. Mat looks at him in utter amazement.

                               MAT
      Have you gone nuts?
Blackie, paying no attention, still looks off.

                               FADE OUT.

FADE IN:

EXT   BURLEY MANSION   DAY
Burley's mansion—on Nob Hill.

                          DISSOLVE TO:

INT   HALLWAY   BURLEY MANSION   BURLEY   MARY BUTLER
Burley is ushering Mary into the hallway. A perfectly trained butler in livery is at the door.

                             BUTLER
    Good afternoon, Mr. Burley.

                           BURLEY
    Good afternoon, Hammond.
Giving butler his hat and cane,

                       BURLEY (cont'd)
    Is my mother here?

BUTLER

She's in the small salon, sir.

BURLEY

Thanks.

BUTLER LEAVES.

BURLEY (cont'd)
(to Mary)

Well—what do you think of our little shack?

Looking about, impressed,

MARY

Why, it's magnificent!

As he starts to lead her off, Mary stops to look at a colossal Chinese vase.

BURLEY

Ah—there's only one *real treasure* in the whole house—and she's waiting to meet you. Come on.

He leads her OFF.

LARGE SALON   MARY   BURLEY

He leads her through the hall into the large impressive salon—Mary further awed by the magnificence and luxury. He ushers Mary into the small salon opening off the large one.

SMALL SALON   MARY   BURLEY   MRS. BURLEY

The salon is exquisitely furnished. Seated playing solitaire in the enclosure of a bay window is Mrs. Burley, known to all San Francisco by her first name, "Maizie." She wears an exquisite lace tea gown and many jewels. O.s. we hear faint, languorous MUSIC of "San Francisco" coming from the house next door, which continues throughout the scene.

BURLEY
(with pride and affection)

Mary—this is my mother.

Mrs. Burley rises.

MRS. BURLEY
(in a marked Irish accent)

How do you do, my dear.
Giving Mrs. Burley her hand,

                    MARY
How do you do?

                    BURLEY
              (to his mother)
Been in all day, Maizie?

                    MRS. BURLEY
No. Sure, I just got back from the races.
She turns—looks at Mary.

                    MRS. BURLEY (cont'd)
You're even prettier close to than you are from me box
at the Tivoli.

                    MARY
              (smiling)
And you are, too!

                    MRS. BURLEY
Go 'long with you!
              (then, to Burley)
You get out!

                    BURLEY
              (amused—surprised)
Get out? *me?*

                    MRS. BURLEY
Certainly *you*! If I have to sell this amazin' beautiful cre-
ature the idea of joining the Burley family—I got to tell
her lies about us that—Heaven forgive me—no son
should hear his mother speak.

                    BURLEY
              (smiling)
All right.
He starts for the door, at which he turns.

BURLEY (cont'd)
Will you send for me when you've made the sale?

MRS. BURLEY
Get out! *Get out!*
BURLEY GOES. Mrs. Burley turns to Mary.

MRS. BURLEY (cont'd)
Sit down, my dear.
Mrs. Burley seats herself beside Mary, facing her—studies her
for a moment.

MRS. BURLEY (cont'd)
Now tell me. Why won't you marry my boy?
Mary hesitates a moment—not wanting to tell Maizie the
truth—finally:

MARY
Mrs. Burley—your family belongs to the *aristocracy* of
San Francisco. I am only the daughter of a poor country
parson. I haven't had the advantages that Jack deserves
in a wife. I'm—

MRS. BURLEY
(cutting in)
Wait a minute, darlin'. I didn't mean what I said just
now about tellin' *lies*. You and I are goin' to speak the
truth to each other.
Mrs. Burley looks right into her face.

MRS. BURLEY (cont'd)
I think I know what it's all about. It's that rapscallion
Blackie Norton you were workin' for down on Pacific
Street!
Mary's lip quivers.

MRS. BURLEY (cont'd)
That boy's left busted hearts all over Frisco—from the
Barbary Coast to Nob Hill!
She thinks a moment—then:

MRS. BURLEY (cont'd)
Listen, Mary, darlin'. I'm an old lady and I've been through a lot in me life. I came to Frisco in the winter of '51 on a sailin' vessel around the Horn. When I got here there were a hundred and fifty men to one female—and if I do say it as shouldn't—I wasn't so hard to look at. I started in business in a shack near Portsmouth Square—doin' washin'. D'you know how long me business lasted?

Mary shakes her head.

MRS. BURLEY (cont'd)
About forty-five minutes!

Then, with a CHUCKLE,

MRS. BURLEY (cont'd)
Me tub was busted to smithereens in a free-for-all fight between five of the town swells—to see which one'd take me to lunch.

Mary smiles . . . A PAUSE . . . Mrs. Burley SIGHS—then:

MRS. BURLEY (cont'd)
(thoughtfully)
So you see—I got to know men!

She pats Mary's shoulder.

MRS. BURLEY (cont'd)
I knew *all kinds* in those early days. And, among 'em I knew a man like Blackie Norton.

Mary looks up sharply.

MRS. BURLEY (cont'd)
Have you ever read those books by a fella named Harte—Bret Harte?

MARY
Yes, I have!

MRS. BURLEY
Well, Harte wrote this fella up in a lot of his stories. Jack Hamlin, he called him.

MARY

Oh, yes! Jack Hamlin—*the gambler*!

MRS. BURLEY

That wasn't his real name of course—
(with a chuckle)
—but Bret Harte got his whole nature *right down pat*!
(reminiscently)
He was a selfish and sinful and Godless and . . . and
beloved scoundrel!

She PAUSES, tears in her eyes, thinking back—then, brushing
the tears away, she takes Mary's hand.

MRS. BURLEY (cont'd)
(softly)
So you see, my dear, I've had my "Blackie Norton" too.

Warmed by her sympathy,

MARY

And you . . . gave him up?

Thinking back—in a reverie,

MRS. BURLEY

Yes. Yes . . . I gave him up—'cause he was killin' my
soul!

MARY
(softly)
Killing your soul, yes. That's it!

A PAUSE—then briskly brushing away her mood,

MRS. BURLEY

So I pulled meself together one day and I married Burley. Burley was a good solid man.
(smiling)
He never got used to *wearing a coat* till the day he
died—but he built me this mansion and every cuspidor
in the place was eighteen karat gold!

Mary LAUGHS.

MRS. BURLEY (cont'd)

And the time came when I was glad I married him, my

dear—'cause he *loved* me—and in a few years Jack was
born and I had me peace!
There is a moment's PAUSE; Mary very thoughtful. Finally:

> MARY
> (impulsively bursting out)
> I *like* you!

> MRS. BURLEY
> (warmly)
> Sure! Sure! We're a couple of regulars—you and me!
> And that's why I can ask you a mighty big favor.

Mary looks up sharply.

> MRS. BURLEY
> Look, Mary—you say we're of the aristocracy of San
> Francisco—and we are. But we haven't got much to
> point with pride to in our past—our way of livin', I
> mean. Life was a bitter struggle in those early days—
> we had to *work hard* and we *did work*! And that took a
> little of the curse off the way we cut loose in our play-
> time—and we *did cut loose*! But this generation *today* in
> San Francisco—ah!

O.s. the languorous MUSIC from next door swells up more
loudly. Mrs. Burley looks off toward the window.

> MRS. BURLEY (cont'd)
> They haven't got to work the way we did. But they're
> *playin'* just as hard—they're playin' harder than we
> did—without anything to balance it off.

Rising,

> MRS. BURLEY (cont'd)
> Come here.

Mary rises—she leads her to the window—gestures off toward
the source of the MUSIC. They look off.

INT/EXT   MC DONOUGH MANSION   MARY'S POV
The house next door from which comes the MUSIC. The blinds
of the house are all down.

MRS. BURLEY (OS)
That's the McDonough mansion. Aristocrats . . . and listen to 'em! They've been carryin' on there for two days and nights straight runnin'. There isn't a rougher joint on the whole Barbary Coast than that "home" right here on Nob Hill.

INT   SMALL SALON   MARY   MRS. BURLEY
Mrs. Burley turns and gestures off in a new direction.

INT/EXT   THE CITY   MARY'S POV
The city which lies below them.

MRS. BURLEY (OS)
They call us the wickedest city in the world. And it's true! The whole town's rotten!

INT   SMALL SALON   MARY   MRS. BURLEY
Mary and Mrs. Burley stand at the window.

MRS. BURLEY
And it's a bitter shame—it is—for deep down underneath all our evil and sin we've got right here in San Francisco *the greatest set of human bein's ever rounded up in one spot!*
She turns—leading Mary back to the couch.

MRS. BURLEY (cont'd)
Sure—they had to have *wild adventure* in their *hearts* and *dynamite* in their *blood* to start out for here in the first place. And they had to laugh at death and danger the whole way—in order to get through! That's why they're so full of untamed deviltry today. But we mustn't go on like we're doin'—blasphemous and sinful and with no feelin' for God in our hearts.
She takes Mary's hand.

MRS. BURLEY (cont'd)
I want my boy to have a good woman, Mary, and raise fine, beautiful kids for the *glory* of our heritage.
A PAUSE—she looks at Mary.

MRS. BURLEY (cont'd)
He's headstrong, my boy is, and a little too proud of his
power. But you can make a fine man of him. And
maybe you'll be glad one day that you met up with the
family of old Maizie Burley—the washer woman.
Smiling—yet very serious,

MARY
I'm glad I know you *now*, Mrs. Burley!

MRS. BURLEY
(correcting her)
Maizie to you, darlin'!

MARY
Maizie.
And then, with a sudden warm, impulsive gesture, she throws
her arms about the old lady.

FADE OUT:

FADE IN:

EXT   PACIFIC STREET   PATROL WAGONS   NIGHT
During the FADE we begin to hear a terrific DIN of GONGS and
POLICE WHISTLES and—then we see a couple of patrol wagons
tearing down Pacific Street. (Night—about 10:30.) CAMERA
PULLS BACK as the first wagon pulls up in front of the
PARADISE, followed by the other. The lobby of the Paradise is
plastered with Blackie's election posters. Denizens of nearby
joints move up to watch as the POLICE jump down off the
wagon.

INT   PARADISE   AUDITORIUM   POLICE
They enter the Paradise. The gambling room is barred off—there
are very few in the audience—but on stage MAT is tearing off a
HOT NUMBER with the ORCHESTRA.

MAT
(singing)
Papa's going to take you to the
Chickens' Ball, A great big ball,
At Lyric Hall.

A CUSTOMER near the door jumps up.

> CUSTOMER
> (calling out)
> The joint's pinched!

Everybody in the audience turns and looks back at the police. On the stage Mat STOPS SINGING—as do the girls. The MUSIC TRAILS OFF. BABE comes out from back stage.

> CAPTAIN
> Come along, everybody. Step along. We haven't got all night, folks.

Mat jumps down off the stage and beats it to a window. A policeman stops Mat.

> POLICEMAN
> Just a moment, pardner!

The policeman grabs Mat.

> POLICEMAN (cont'd)
> What you doin'?

At the window,

> MAT
> It's close in here.

> POLICEMAN
> It'll be closer where you're going.

He starts to drag him off. BLACKIE approaches the Captain.

> BLACKIE
> Good evening, Charlie.

> CAPTAIN
> Good evening. Sorry I have to do this, Blackie.

Babe barges up to listen.

> BLACKIE
> What's the charge?

> CAPTAIN
> Serving liquor without a license.

> BABE
> (indignant—cutting in)
> We've got a license.

> CAPTAIN
> It's been revoked.

Blackie smiles bitterly, then:

> BLACKIE
> (thoughtfully)
> What'll the rap be, Charlie?

> CAPTAIN
> Probably five thousand fine, or a year in jail. You know
> Judge Corrigan.

> BLACKIE
> (quizzically)
> Yeah—I know him. But Burley knows him better!

> CAPTAIN
> I'd like to help you, Blackie—but you know I've got a
> wife and kids to take care of.

> BLACKIE
> I understand—but look, Charlie, I've been counting on
> winning that prize money at the Chickens' Ball. Will
> you give me a couple of hours to rustle up bail—get my
> entertainers out?

The Captain PAUSES, then:

> CAPTAIN
> (in assent)
> Be at the station before six in the morning.

> BLACKIE
> Thanks.

Suddenly tough—the Captain turns on Babe.

> CAPTAIN
> Come on, you!

Saying which, he roughly hustles him OUT. Blackie follows.

EXT PARADISE POLICE OTHERS
The lobby is now crowded—a semi-circle of denizens of the
Coast looking on in awe and SILENCE as the police hustle their
prisoners into the wagons.

POLICE
Step along there!
Get a move on, sister!
Step lively! (etc.)

BLACKIE stands under a campaign poster of himself—looking
off toward the wagons—doing some quick thinking as to bail,
when—

HARLAN (OS)
Well, Blackie! Had enough?

Blackie looks up. KENNETH HARLAN in a plain business suit
ENTERS THE SHOT.

BLACKIE
Hello. What's *eating* you?

HARLAN
We can't beat Burley, Blackie!

BLACKIE
So he's got you buffaloed, has he?

HARLAN
It's tough, but if we trail with you, we'll get what
you're gettin'. And none of us can afford to be raided.
(significantly)
I'm not here on my own—the boys *sent* me.

Blackie reacts to the desertion of his backers—then:

BLACKIE
(stubbornly valiant)
The district's full of little mugs who are counting on me
to go through for 'em. And I'm going through.

Beginning to be exasperated,

HARLAN
You haven't done any business since they started raid-

ing you. How'll you get the dough to carry on your campaign?

     BLACKIE
    (enthusiastic)
Look, whoever wins that ten thousand tonight could carry us clear through the campaign!

     HARLAN
    (with significance)
Not if *I* win it!

     BLACKIE
    (quickly)
Why not? It'll be a great investment! We'll build a *new* Coast that'll top anything Frisco's ever known!

     HARLAN
The old Coast's been pretty good to me, Blackie! And it's been all right to *you*—up to now!

     BLACKIE
Well, I'm not going to quit!

     HARLAN
    (significantly)
Are you fighting for the *Coast*, or are you fighting Burley for a *personal* reason?
Blackie looks at him.

    HARLAN (cont'd)
    (with finality)
We think it's personal, Blackie. We've had a bellyful of this "boudoir" battle.
He turns and walks away, Blackie watching after. The police wagons are now heading away from the front of the place. The onlookers begin to disperse. Blackie looks off dazedly.

     CAPTAIN (OS)
Want anything from inside, Blackie?
As Blackie looks up, the CAPTAIN is heading for the front door, a padlock in his hand.

                    BLACKIE
            (grimly—quizzically)
        I might put out the lights.

                    CAPTAIN
        That's right.
The Captain LAUGHS.

                CAPTAIN (cont'd)
        No use running up your light bill.
Blackie heads to the door.

INT PARADISE
BLACKIE comes into the Paradise, goes to the switch box near the door. The auditorium is now deserted. One by one Blackie turns off the switches until the place is lit only from the street light coming in the open door. Blackie turns and goes back to the now darkened lobby.

EXT PARADISE CAPTAIN
BLACKIE COMES OUT. He watches as the Captain is putting the padlock on the door.

                    BLACKIE
        That's the first time the joint's ever been locked. We threw away the key the night it opened.

                    CAPTAIN
            (touched—kindly)
        See you before six, Blackie.
The CAPTAIN GOES OFF. As Blackie stands thinking about bail—

                NEWSBOY (OS)
        Papers! Here you are—just out—morning papers!
Blackie turns and heads through the darkened and deserted lobby for the street down which comes the NEWSBOY.

                    NEWSBOY
            (warmly)
        Hello, Blackie.
Blackie's heading on his way.

                    BLACKIE

Hello, Bill.
The newsboy runs along beside him—thrusts a paper at him.

                    NEWSBOY
          Have a paper!

                    BLACKIE
          Thanks.
Blackie takes out a half dollar.

                    NEWSBOY
          Aw—it's on me, tonight!

                    BLACKIE
              (touched)
          Thanks.
The NEWSBOY DROPS BEHIND. At which point a picture on the
front page suddenly attracts Blackie's interest. He stops short,
an expression of shock on his face.

INSERT   NEWSPAPER
The front of the paper—on which we see date, APRIL 17, 1906.
Headlines reading:
          JACK BURLEY ENGAGED TO DIVA.
          Scion of old San Francisco family to wed Mary Blake of
          the Tivoli.
Under the headlines is a large photograph of Mary, her head
only.
                                        DISSOLVE TO:

INT   CLOSE SHOT   TIVOLI STAGE   MARY   NIGHT
During the DISSOLVE we hear Mary SINGING, hitting a long,
high note. Now we see her SINGING. CAMERA PULLS BACK to
reveal Mary at the finale of *Traviata* (or *Manon*). She SINGS
through to a brilliant, rousing finish.

AUDIENCE AND STAGE   MARY
The Tivoli Opera House is crowded on the last night of the sea-
son. They start to APPLAUD. Mary acknowledging applause—

bows her way OFF. Curtain falls. APPLAUSE continues louder than before.

STAGE BOX   BURLEY   MRS. BURLEY   OTHERS
Burley, Mrs. Burley, and four other socialites APPLAUDING. Burley proud, beaming.

BOX   FREDDY DUANE
At the front of the box sits Freddy Duane and another party of socialites—Freddy a little tight, APPLAUDING.

STAGE   MARY
She comes out and bows. The audience o.s. APPLAUDS even more violently.

ORCHESTRA   TIM
Father Tim, seated alone, APPLAUDING enthusiastically.

STAGE   MARY
She bows her way OFF.

AUDIENCE
The APPLAUSE INCREASES.

STAGE   MARY
She comes out again.

AUDIENCE
The audience goes wild. People call out.

PEOPLE IN AUDIENCE
        Speech! Speech!

STAGE   MARY
Mary, overcome with emotion and gratitude, steps forward. The APPLAUSE dies down.

                    MARY
                (from her heart)
        Thank you. This season of the Tivoli has made me very
        happy. I've learned to love San Francisco—it's going to
        be my home!
She smiles at Burley in his box.

AUDIENCE
The audience LAUGHS and looking up at Burley, APPLAUDS him.

STAGE BOX   BURLEY   MRS. BURLEY
Mrs. Burley nudges Burley to rise.

MRS. BURLEY
Get up, you numbskull!
Burley, beaming, rises and acknowledges the APPLAUSE. Finally, he resumes his seat.

STAGE   MARY
As the APPLAUSE for Burley dies down, Mary winds up her speech.

MARY
I hope you'll let me sing for you next year.

AUDIENCE AND STAGE   MARY
Again the house goes wild. Cries from the audience:

PEOPLE IN AUDIENCE
You bet we will. You belong to Frisco now! We love you, Mary.
Mary kisses her hand to the audience several times and then, tossing a last happy kiss toward Burley's box, goes OFF. The curtain falls.

DISSOLVE TO:

BACKSTAGE   STAGE HANDS
The stage hands hop to it to remove the scenery.

THE WINGS   BALDINI   MARY
Baldini waiting in the wings grabs Mary in a comradelike caress and kisses her heartily on each cheek.

BURLEY (OS)
(kiddingly jealous)
Just a moment there!
BURLEY ENTERS THE SCENE, grabs Mary and whirls her around.

Burley looks down on her, aglow with pride—Mary looking happily up into his face—her eyes shining.

                    BURLEY
        I love you!

                    MARY
        I'm glad!

                    ATTENDANT (OS)
        Mr. Burley!
As they look up, a House ATTENDANT ENTERS SHOT.

                    ATTENDANT
            (happily—in suppressed excitement)
        The caterers are here from the Poodle Dog Restaurant.

                    BURLEY
        Good! Tell them to bring the tables on the stage!

                    ATTENDANT
        Yes, sir.
The ATTENDANT hurries away.

                    MARY
        Better go look after things, dear.

                    BURLEY
        You're right.
He flicks her chin.

                    BURLEY (cont'd)
        As usual.
He turns to go.

                    MARY
        Oh, wait.
He stops.

                    MARY (cont'd)
        You forgot to ask the stage hands to the banquet.
Never having even thought of it,

> BURLEY

Did I?

> MARY

I asked them.

> BURLEY

Darling!

He gives her a quick kiss and hurries OFF. Mary turns and starts for her dressing room. She passes through the bustle of the CAST scurrying to their dressing rooms—WAITERS carrying in the long banquet tables, chairs, cases of champagne, etc., etc. O.s. backstage NOISES—the ORCHESTRA—a SINGER singing snatches of song with it—etc.

CORRIDOR OUTSIDE DRESSING ROOM   MARY
At the end of a corridor Mary reaches her dressing room door where she sees TIM waiting for her. She hurries to him.

> MARY
> (from her heart)

Father Mullin!

> TIM

Mary!

They shake hands warmly. There is a moment's PAUSE as they look at each other—then:

> MARY

Were you out front tonight?

> TIM

Your *last* night?

> MARY

I'm glad one of the . . . one of the old gang still re-members me.

Beginning to study her,

> TIM

I got my invitation to your wedding, Mary.

                    MARY
        And will you come?
Tim still studies her.

                     TIM
        Of course!
A STAGE HAND steps up excitedly—a champagne cocktail in his
hand.

                STAGE HAND
        Everybody's going to the Green Room, Miss Blake—for
        champagne!

                    MARY
        Thanks, Herman.
With a big grin, the stage hand holds out his glass.

                STAGE HAND
        I got mine!
They LAUGH. The STAGE HAND goes on OFF. A PAUSE—Tim
looks at her, then:

                     TIM
        Are you happy, Mary?
Looking right into his eyes,

                    MARY
                (a trace overemphatic)
        Yes!
Not at all convinced,

                     TIM
        Then everything's all right.
Tim takes her hand.

                TIM (cont'd)
        Good night, my dear.

                    MARY
        Won't you join our supper party?

                     TIM
        Sorry—but I've got to be running along.

MARY
(a trace sadly)
Good night.

His heart aching for her,

TIM
God bless you.

TIM LEAVES. Mary looks after him—SIGHS a little sigh—then turns and goes into her dressing room.

DRESSING ROOM   MARY

Mary's maid is busily arranging things for her to change. Mary, preoccupied, thoughtful, goes to the mirror, starting to remove her headdress when o.s. there's a KNOCK on the door.

MARY
Come in.

BURLEY opens the door.

BURLEY
(hectically happy)
They're calling for you, dear.

MARY
But I've got to change.

BURLEY
Don't bother now! You can change before the ball.

MARY
The ball?

BURLEY
Sure. We're going to wind up at the Chickens' Ball!

Mary PAUSES, then:

MARY
Oh, no, Jack.

BURLEY
Why not?

Mary looks at him—he reads her expression—then—with an understanding smile:

BURLEY (cont'd)
Aw—that's all right, dear! I happen to know that Blackie Norton won't be there!

As she looks up at him,

DISSOLVE TO:

EXT   CLOSE SHOT   LYRIC HALL   SIGN   NIGHT
The sign on Lyric Hall reads:

ANNUAL CHICKENS' BALL—APRIL 17th, 1906
Master of Ceremonies
Mr. Freddy Duane

The CAMERA PANS DOWN and picks up BLACKIE as he makes
his way into the Hall. O.s. the HOT RHYTHM of a specialty
number BLARING out from the hall on the second floor.

STAIRS   BLACKIE   OTHERS
As Blackie hurries upstairs, colorful types from the Coast greet
him and then look speculatively after him.

COAST TYPES
Hello, Blackie.
Good evening, Blackie.
H'Yah, Blackie.

BLACKIE acknowledges their greetings as he hurries on into the
hall.

INT   LYRIC HALL   CROWD
The Hall is crowded with types of all kinds—people from
Chinatown and the Barbary Coast, on up to swells in evening
dress and jewels. They are seated at small tables around the
edge of the main floor and around a horse-shoe balcony, drinking. In b.g. on the stage a Rathskeller TRIO is just starting. On a
pedestal at one side of the stage is the silver cup with its contents of gold pieces. On the other side of the stage is an easel on
which stands a large card reading: PRESENTED BY ALASKA JOE
KELSO OF THE HIPPODROME. Part of the crowd is milling about
visiting between tables, the underworld characters mixing in
with those of Nob Hill.

FIRST TABLE   BARBARY COAST TYPES
Several obvious Barbary Coast types, men and girls watch the

performance of the Rathskeller NUMBER o.s. An exquisitely gowned SOCIETY WOMAN moves up, a glass of champagne in her hand. She stops, signalling to one of the men, a very handsome type in a turtle-neck sweater. Holding out her glass toward the man,

> SOCIETY WOMAN
> Drink up, Sport.

The Coast type man looks up, sees her, and delighted, rises.

> COAST TYPE
> Sure thing.

They drink.

> COAST TYPE (cont'd)
> What's your name?

> SOCIETY WOMAN
> What does it matter?

> COAST TYPE
> (apologetically)
> That's right.

Saying which, he grabs her and kisses her. The others at the table pay no attention to them.

ANOTHER TABLE   SOCIETY PEOPLE
A group of society people are seated at this table. A MIDDLE-AGED SOCIETY MAN is carrying a pretty girl up to the table. She is half-dressed in a stage costume and is GIGGLING.

> MIDDLE-AGED SOCIETY MAN
> (to those at table)
> Look what I found in a dressing room.

They LAUGH. The girl GIGGLES. A WOMAN who sits with her arm around the neck of a handsome man:

> WOMAN
> (to girl)
> I can recommend him, honey. He's my husband.

The girl GIGGLES again and the man sits down at the table with her in his lap.

BURLEY'S TABLE   MARY   BURLEY
Mary and Burley are seated with a man and woman. They are all
very gay, drinking champagne and looking off, highly amused
at the show. O.s. the NOISE and MUSIC of entertainment continue. Everyone and everything is very gay and in key with the
hectic surroundings. Mary is exaggeratedly, almost hectically,
gay—pretending even to herself that she is happy.

> BURLEY
> (to Mary amusedly)
> Bet you fifty dollars this is the winning act!

> MARY
> (laughingly—kiddingly—as if in challenge)
> I'll put fifty on the act before this!

> BURLEY
> All right, sweetheart. If you lose—I'll pay your bet.

He takes her hand—kisses it. She smiles and looks off toward
the stage.

STAGE   RATHSKELLER TRIO   MARY'S POV
On stage dancers perform a CAKE WALK routine.

BURLEY'S TABLE   MARY   BURLEY   WAITER
Burley turns to a waiter.

> BURLEY
> (genially)
> Clear this away, will you, and bring us a whole new set
> up.

> WAITER
> You bet, sir!

Proceeding to clear away the glasses, he turns to Mary.

> WAITER (cont'd)
> Ain't you that new star at the Tivoli?

> MARY
> Yes.

> WAITER
> (to Burley)

> If I had a girl making that kind of dough, *I'd* buy wine,
> too.

Saying which, he winks at Burley. They all LAUGH and look off
at the stage.

DELLA'S TABLE   DELLA   POMPOUS MAN
Della sits with a pompous-looking man. She looks off toward
the entrance through which we see BLACKIE ENTERING. Della
rises. Signaling Blackie,

              DELLA
       Oh, Blackie!

Blackie in b.g. sees Della and makes his way toward her through
the crowd. Colorful types greet him as he goes and then look
speculatively after him.

              DELLA
          (to pompous man)
       Beat it, will you?

              POMPOUS MAN
       All right, Della.

He rises and LEAVES. As Blackie reaches the table,

              DELLA
       How about it, kid? Did you get 'em out?

              BLACKIE
       They're being held without bail.

Della reacts—sore—beginning to smoulder:

              DELLA
       Without bail? . . .

She looks o.s. and sees Mary and Burley.

              DELLA (cont'd)
          (bitterly)
       There they are now, celebrating.

Without even looking,

              BLACKIE
          (casually)
       Are they?

DELLA

He won't be satisfied until you're under a wet rock.
Why don't you go over and curl that dude's mustache,
and I'll kiss the lady with a bottle.

Blackie LAUGHS. Then, brushing aside the whole matter,

BLACKIE
(gamely)

Aw, forget it . . . Thanks just the same, Della. You're a
sweetheart if there ever was one.

Blackie reaches in his pocket, takes out a handful of rings, starts
to put them on her fingers. Della looks at him dazedly. Blackie
looks at one ring.

BLACKIE (cont'd)

Didn't *I* give you this one?

DELLA
(still dazed)

Yeah—you were just a kid!

BLACKIE
(smiling)

That's right.

At which point o.s. ENTHUSIASTIC APPLAUSE. Blackie looks off
at the stage.

STAGE   RATHSKELLER TRIO   BLACKIE'S POV
We show the high spot of the Rathskeller number, which finally
finishes.

AUDIENCE
The audience breaks into LOUD APPLAUSE.

DELLA'S TABLE   BLACKIE   DELLA
Blackie turns from the stage toward Della.

BLACKIE

A pretty fair number. It may get Red Kelly the prize.

Blackie rises.

DELLA
(thoughtful—preoccupied)

Where you going, Blackie?

                    BLACKIE
Over to my place. I've got to pack up a few things.
Della starts to rise.

                    DELLA
I'll go help you.

                    BLACKIE
No, you won't.
He pushes her back.

                    BLACKIE (cont'd)
See the show and come over later. You can tell me who
won.

                    DELLA
          (heartsick)
They say you'll go up for a year, Blackie!

                    BLACKIE
Aw—I can handle it! I'm worried about the others.

                    DELLA
          (from her heart)
If the women had a vote, kid—you'd be next *governor*!
Blackie smiles—pinches her cheek and LEAVES. Della looks
after Blackie a moment—reacts in sympathy to him—then turns
and makes a bee line for Burley's table.

BURLEY'S TABLE   MARY   BURLEY
Burley, seated next to Mary, is holding her hand on top of the
table. DELLA briskly barges up.

                    DELLA
Good evening, folks.
They look up.

                    DELLA (cont'd)
D'you mind if I sit down.
By which time she is already seated.

MARY
(a trace constrainedly)
I'm glad to see you, Della.

DELLA
You won't be for long!
They all react—surprised.

DELLA (cont'd)
I just dropped over to tell you what I think of you!
She turns to Burley's astonished guests.

DELLA (cont'd)
I haven't seen the woman since she walked out on the best man in San Francisco to marry the town's number one rodent!
As if thinking her tight,

BURLEY
(warningly)
I think you'd better go, Della.

DELLA
Oh, no. I've got a few things to say to you, too.
Again turning to the guests,

DELLA (cont'd)
In case you folks don't follow me I'll tell you that this mouse here—
Della indicates Burley.

DELLA (cont'd)
—has just had a padlock put on the Paradise and thrown all Blackie Norton's performers in jail!
Mary starts.

DELLA (cont'd)
(her voice rising)
That's what Blackie got for picking this phony up out of the gutter and giving her a chance. She waltzed out on him and had Burley slip him the works! Blackie's broke.

He hasn't got a dime and he'll be sent to the pen for probably a year!
Della indicates Burley and Mary.

DELLA (cont'd)
Delightful people!
Burley turns to his guests, not even trying to cover his fury.

BURLEY
Come on, folks!
Burley starts to rise. Della pushes him right back into his chair.

DELLA
Hold still!
Della rises.

DELLA (cont'd)
Don't think I'm going to breathe the air *near you* any longer than I have to!
(to Mary)
You ought to make that mouse awfully happy!
Della planks a five-dollar gold piece down on the table.

DELLA (cont'd)
(to Burley)
Here's a five spot, brother. I'm buying back my introduction to you.
Saying which, DELLA sails on OUT of the scene. They all look after her—Mary stunned—dazed.

DUANE (OS)
Ladies and gentlemen.

STAGE AND AUDIENCE   DUANE
Duane holds the center of the stage—his watch in his hand.

DUANE
The last entry of the evening was to have been from Mr. Blackie Norton's Paradise—
Then, in reference to Blackie's arrest:

DUANE (cont'd)
(quizzically)

but as it is now *four-thirty* and Mr. Norton's performers
have failed to arrive—
There's a BUZZ of amused comment which goes up from the
audience.

> DUANE (cont'd)
> we'll close the contest without them.

LOUD APPLAUSE from Alaska's adherents, one of whom rises.

BURLEY'S TABLE   MARY   BURLEY
Mary rises and:

> MARY
> (calls out)
> Mr. Duane! I'm representing the Paradise for Mr. Nor-
> ton!

In b.g. we see people react amazed at Mary's action. Burley rises
and, so as not to be heard:

> BURLEY
> (very quietly)
> I forbid you to go up there!

Making no reaction to his words—chin up and shoulders
squared, Mary starts down through the crowd toward the stage.

DELLA'S TABLE   MARY   DELLA
Mary passes Della on her way to the stage. Della rises, looking
after Mary in surprise and admiration as MARY HEADS OFF toward the stage. She watches a moment—then, getting a sudden
idea—turns excitedly.

> DELLA
> (calls)
> Oh Dave!

DAVE, a man who stands nearby gaping off at Mary, turns and
looks at Della.

> DELLA (cont'd)
> Know where Blackie Norton lives?

> DAVE
> Sure.

DELLA
(almost in exultation)
Go get him!

DAVE
You bet.

Dave turns and GOES OFF. O.s. APPLAUSE for Mary grows.

THE STAGE   DUANE   MARY
The APPLAUSE now general—members of the audience begin to call for "San Francisco."

AUDIENCE MEMBERS (OS)
San Francisco!

The demand steadily increases. Mary heads up the steps at the side of the stage. Duane takes her by the arm, escorts her to center of stage, holds up his hand for silence. The APPLAUSE o.s. dies down.

DUANE
Ladies and gentlemen—representing the Paradise—Miss Mary Blake.

AUDIENCE
The audience APPLAUDS LOUDER.

                    AUDIENCE
                (calls for number)
            San Francisco!

ORCHESTRA PIT   ORCHESTRA LEADER
The orchestra leader TAPPING for attention, starts the INTRO-
DUCTION to the song.

STAGE   MARY
Mary begins to SING "San Francisco," singing alone.

BURLEY'S TABLE   BURLEY
He watches—dazed.

STAGE   MARY
Mary finishes SINGING once through and begins again—this
time people in the audience o.s. begin to join in—one by one.

BURLEY'S TABLE
Burley reacts.

AUDIENCE   VARIOUS TYPES
Various types in the audience as they join enthusiastically in
SONG.

STAGE   MARY
Mary begins the third rendition of "San Francisco." By this time
the entire audience is SINGING with her. Mary SINGS—her
voice rising in obligato above them all. Mary finishes the song
on a thrilling high note.

AUDIENCE
The audience goes wild.

                                        DISSOLVE TO:

STAGE   DUANE   MARY   OTHERS
The leading contestants are lined up in a row. Duane is pointing
to each contestant in turn and the audience retaliates with
APPLAUSE. Alaska's entrants who stand next to Mary get tremendous APPLAUSE, but when Duane comes to Mary at the end

of the line she gets a positive OVATION. During the wild
APPLAUSE:

HALL ENTRANCE   BLACKIE   DELLA
We see Blackie just entering the hall with Della who is trying to
hold him back.

STAGE   DUANE   MARY
Duane holds up his hand to stop the applause. Then:

                    DUANE
        Ladies and gentlemen. The appearance of Miss Blake
        for the Paradise was as great a surprise to me as it was
        to you.

HALL ENTRANCE   BLACKIE   DELLA
Blackie reacts—his face white with fury. Della watches him.

                    DUANE (OS)
        I congratulate you on your choice and present the
        award to Miss Blake for Mr. Blackie Norton—together
        with my congratulations.

STAGE   DUANE
Duane turns to pick up the cup with its contents of gold pieces.
At which point:

                    BLACKIE (OS)
        Just a moment there!
Everybody looks o.s. at Blackie.

HALL ENTRANCE   BLACKIE   DELLA
Blackie, breaking away from Della, heads for the stage.

                    BLACKIE
        There's been a mistake here, Mr. Duane.

STAGE   MARY   DUANE
Mary and Duane look at BLACKIE as he runs up the steps onto
the stage. Gesturing toward Mary contemptuously,

                    BLACKIE
                (to Duane)
        I never told that woman she could appear for me!

Mary looks at him, aghast.

AUDIENCE
A GASP goes up from the crowd.

STAGE   BLACKIE   MARY   DUANE
Blackie turns, takes the cup by its base and faces Mary.

> BLACKIE
> You've got me all wrong, sister. I don't need this kind
> of dough!

Saying which he throws the cup at her feet—the gold pieces
CLATTERING all over the stage—and then BLACKIE heads down
the platform.

AUDIENCE AND STAGE   CROWD   BLACKIE
There is a moment's dazed SILENCE as the crowd looks up at the
stage—after which it breaks out in LOUD EXCLAMATIONS—
BOOING Blackie as he makes his way toward the exit.

> PEOPLE IN CROWD
> You're pretty cheap, Blackie!
> That's *rotten*, Blackie!
> This isn't the Bowery—it's *Frisco*!

STAGE   MARY   DUANE   OTHERS
Mary stands rooted to the floor. Duane stepping forward addresses Alaska's entrants.

> DUANE
> I guess that prize belongs to you, boys.

Alaska's entrants hop to it and start to retrieve the coins.

AUDIENCE   MASTER OF CEREMONIES   CROWD
In order to close the incident,

> MASTER OF CEREMONIES
> (calls)
> *Everybody stew!*

Meaning dance. The orchestra starts to PLAY "After the Ball."
The crowd makes for the dance floor. MARY comes down off the
stage. She is humiliated, stunned. She walks along the wall,
thinking only to escape further humiliation. People look at her

sympathetically and WHISPER to each other. As she walks along, BURLEY suddenly confronts her. There is a pause of embarrassment. Finally:—

BURLEY
(quietly—gently—loverlike)
Do you want me to take you home, Mary?

Mary PAUSES, then:

MARY
(softly—gratefully—from her heart)
Yes, Jack.

Burley puts his arm about her and starts to lead her off.

HALL ENTRANCE   BURLEY   MARY
Burley leads Mary down a short flight of steps toward the door leading into the ballroom. O.s. there's a strange, LOW, PROTRACTED RUMBLE. They stop. The RUMBLE INCREASES.

BALLROOM   CROWD
The dancing crowd is jamming the floor. A number of them look up, listening to the ominous RUMBLE, then stop.

HALL ENTRANCE   MARY   BURLEY
They are at the door leading through to the ballroom.

BURLEY
It's an explosion! Must be a boiler some place.

He opens the door to escort Mary through and starts to close the door when right before their eyes the door frame with a LOUD CREAKING of wood shifts out of plumb so that the door no longer fits. Mary looks at Burley in questioning alarm.

BURLEY
It's an earthquake!

They turn and look out over the hall.

THE HALL   MARY   BURLEY   BLACKIE   OTHERS
Mary and Burley in f.g. In b.g. Blackie stands by the front wall. The floor directly in f.g. shakes violently, toppling tables, chairs and people. Dancers are tripped up. A large chandelier in the f.g. drops several feet and remains swinging, hanging by the

electric wire that holds it. Behind Blackie with a great CRACK-LING of bricks and plaster, two wide parallel cracks speed their way up the wall from floor to ceiling. The floor settling causes the portion of the wall between the two wide cracks to fall forward. Blackie, among others, is felled by a large chunk of the wall. The crowd SCREAMS. Mary—frantic—struggles with Burley.

> MARY
>
> Blackie! Blackie!

> BURLEY
>
> Come on! It's too late!

He drags her off toward the exit, Mary still struggling to get away to Blackie. The crowd, in pandemonium, heads for the exit. Debris and a shower of plaster keep dropping. The chandelier swings wildly. O.s. the SCREAMS of the crowd, the CRACKLING of glass and masonry and the RUMBLE of the earth itself. A woman's voice can be heard above the noise:

> WOMAN (OS)
> (frantically screaming out)
> Bill! Where are you? Bill!

> ANOTHER PERSON (OS)
>
> Look out for the chandelier!

Mary and Burley—swept along by the crowd—Mary so packed in that she is no longer able to struggle. In an anguish of prayer,

> MARY
>
> Oh, God, save him!

As they near the exit o.s. a terrific WRENCHING SOUND. They look up in terror. A portion of the balcony near the exit wrenches loose and CRASHES. Mary goes limp. Burley picks her up in his arms and goes on. The SCREEN is obliterated in a haze of dust and powdered plaster.

> DISSOLVE TO:

MONTAGE—CITY HALL

The light is dim, as at 5 A.M. People are rushing from all directions into the street as the stone work and dome on the City Hall crash down with a THUNDEROUS NOISE.

MONTAGE—POODLE DOG RESTAURANT
People mowing each other down in their efforts to escape from the building.

MONTAGE—LOTTA'S FOUNTAIN
The fountain is in f.g.; in b.g. we see a big office building collapse after which there is an EXPLOSION as of a boiler and a cloud of smoke goes up.

MONTAGE—BUSINESS STREET
Office and street are deserted at this hour. Walls of some buildings fall—others are just warped.

MONTAGE—RESIDENCE STREET
In the poor quarter some of the frame buildings are leaning forward toward the street. The occupants, in night clothes, are running out of the houses. Several women kneel in the street, praying. A milk truck, driverless, drawn by two crazed horses, plunges down the street, the milk cans crashing as it goes. END OF MONTAGE. (During the above montage, we see quick flashes in CLOSE SHOTS of terrified people in the action indicated. Also, during the montage, the morning light gradually increases.)

EXT   LYRIC HALL   PEOPLE   MORNING
The milk truck plunges through, people scrambling wildly to get out of the way of it on the street. The scene is one of pandemonium. Many of the revellers have reached the street. Some of them keep on running, others stand dazed, many JITTERING incoherently. Still others are looking about SCREAMING for loved ones lost in the melee. Through the entrance of Lyric Hall, partly blocked by fallen masonry, a jam of half-crazed humanity is still struggling to get out. BLACKIE emerges through the crowd jammed in the exit, dishevelled, dusty with powdered plaster, a big bleeding gash in his forehead. Even in the pandemonium he is able to over-ride the crowd, pushing his way through, trying to find Mary. Blackie looks about through the crowd, SCREAMING OUT, violent, almost vicious in his importunity:

BLACKIE
Mary! Where are you! Mary!

He reaches the street and grabs a member of the orchestra, a
MUSICIAN, who stands dazedly, grasping the broken end of a
cello.

> BLACKIE (cont'd)
> Have you seen Mary Blake?

> MUSICIAN
> (dazed)
> I saw her start out—with Burley.

Blackie goes on into the street among the escaping revellers.

> BLACKIE
> (calling out, violently, in staccato)
> Mary! Mary!

At which point he suddenly stops, looking down. BURLEY lies
dead in the street, the sign of Lyric Hall lying on him. Blackie
stands looking at Burley a moment then, in utter anguish over
Mary's possible fate,

> BLACKIE
> (screams out more violent than ever)
> Mary! Mary!

At which point we hear o.s. the terrific RUMBLE of a second
earthquake shock. Right at Blackie's feet, the street heaves up,
cracks, and drops about four or five feet. Many are thrown to the
ground by the impact. O.s. SCREAMS OF TERROR over which
can be heard:

> WOMAN (OS)
> Oh God! Oh God have mercy on us.

Also o.s. a ROAR of cracking masonry. Blackie, struggling to
keep his feet, looks off.

HOTEL   BLACKIE'S POV
A three-story hotel across from Lyric Hall. The walls are cracking and presently the entire face of the building falls out and
crumples into the street below. In one of the rooms we see a
MOTHER frantically picking up a CHILD thrown to the floor. In
another room a MAN is holding onto a bed, halfway dropping
off the building. The bed rolls on out and he falls out after it. In

other rooms we see people frantically backing away from the
opening, or running in terror along the corridor.

STREET   BLACKIE   OTHERS
Blackie, among others, is looking on in terror at the above. O.s.
SCREAMS—CALLS of "Help" from people who are trapped—
GROANS of the injured and dying, NOISE of falling masonry
and showers of plaster. Above everything we hear one woman's
shrill voice calling out:

> WOMAN (OS)
> It's the end of the world! It's the end of the world!

> OTHERS (OS)
> Keep away from the buildings! Get to an open space!

People now start a fairly concentrated movement—running
frantically down the middle of the street to escape falling
masonry, but a few drop to their knees in prayer, among them
RED KELLY. Blackie calls out into the rapidly dispersing crowd,
frantic to learn if Mary is among them. As Blackie moves along,

> BLACKIE
> *Mary! Mary!*

He comes upon Red Kelly who is JITTERING a prayer—almost
inaudible in the frightful DIN. Blackie grabs Kelly's shoulder.

> BLACKIE
> (violently)
> Have you seen Mary Blake?

Kelly, paying no attention, goes right on:

> RED KELLY
> I have been a sinner, oh Lord! Forgive me!

Shaking him viciously,

> BLACKIE
> Stop that drivel and help me find Mary Blake!

> RED KELLY
> Let me alone!

Shaking himself free of Blackie's hold, he goes right on MUM-
BLING, almost inaudible:

RED KELLY (cont'd)
I've been a sinner! Oh Lord, forgive me. Oh Lord, forgive me!

Blackie gives him a push and starts off when FREDDY DUANE
APPEARS, helping one of the colored CAKE WALKERS who has
been injured and is limping.

BLACKIE
(calls to him)
Have you seen Mary Blake?

Duane, looking up, sees Blackie.

DUANE
I saw her with Burley. They got out!

Duane moves on. Blackie looks after him—stunned.

DUANE (cont'd)
Try her hotel, Blackie. She may go there.

BLACKIE
(dazed—calls after him)
Where is it?

DUANE
The Grenoble—on Bush Street.

Blackie goes on, making his way over the debris, when suddenly he stops, looking down. A woman's bare arm sticks out from
under the debris. Blackie, sick with fear that it is Mary, stoops,
wrenching aside a piece of broken beam which covers the woman, and reveals her face. It is DELLA—dead. Blackie looks at her
a moment—stunned—dazed—then chastened by the death of
Della, a trace less violent, beginning to lose something of his
vicious importunity but none the less frantic, he hurriedly
makes his way on over the debris.

DISSOLVE TO:

STREET   BLACKIE   OTHERS

Blackie is going down the street a little distance from Lyric Hall.
In b.g. we see a few REFUGEES making their way along over the
debris, some with suitcases. Blackie passes a broken gas main
sticking up out of a fissure, a strange HISSING SOUND coming

from it. Stopping a REFUGEE, still violent but a little more thoughtful than when we saw him last:

> BLACKIE
> Have you seen a red-haired girl in a white ball dress?

> REFUGEE
> Haven't seen her, pal.

The refugee indicates the broken gas main.

> REFUGEE (cont'd)
> Better look out! That gas main's broken!

The refugee goes OFF. Blackie stands dazed.

> CHICK (OS)
> (whimpering)
> Holy Virgin—Oh Holy Virgin help me.

Blackie turns—looks off.

> BLACKIE
> (calling off)
> Chick!

Then we see CHICK stumbling along, whimpering.

> BLACKIE (cont'd)
> Have you seen Mary Blake?

> CHICK
> (whimpering—despairing)
> No. I've lost my old lady, Blackie!

Blackie looks at him, the spectacle of this big mug whimpering like a child further touches and chastens him. Showing his first interest in someone else,

> BLACKIE
> Maybe she went home.

> CHICK
> (whimpering)
> I can't find her! My house is in the street!

CHICK GOES ON OFF—at which point:

> MAN (OS)
> (screaming)

Look out for live wires!
Blackie looks up. A telegraph pole, half leaning, starts slowly to fall, dragging with it a tangle of wires which emit sparks on hitting the trolley rails. Blackie jumps back from the gas main, just as the live wire strikes it. There is an EXPLOSION as the gas ignites, making a blinding glare, followed by a puff of black smoke which blots out the SCREEN.

DISSOLVE TO:

LOTTA'S FOUNTAIN
BLACKIE COMES INTO THE SHOT. He is breathless from his laborious journey on foot over the debris, his clothing torn and blackened. The building in which we saw the explosion earlier is now a roaring furnace. From a fissure in the street the water from a broken main is gushing like a geyser. In b.g. REFUGEES are already heading down the street carrying hastily rescued goods of all descriptions, some dragging baby carriages, toy wagons, etc. A fire engine dashes down the street over the debris and pulls up near Blackie, by a hydrant. A fireman rushes to the hydrant.

BLACKIE
(out of breath—to the fireman)
Is the Grenoble Hotel all right—on Bush Street?
The fireman, busy at the hydrant, doesn't hear, at which point a MAN runs in, pushing right past Blackie.

MAN
(screaming to fireman)
My house is on fire!

SECOND FIREMAN
Where is it?

MAN
Four blocks down—on Folsom.
By which time, both firemen have unscrewed the cap off the hydrant and turned on the water revealing a mere trickle. A third fireman at the hydrant:

THIRD FIREMAN
(to First Fireman)

No use, Boss.
The Third Fireman jumps back on the fire engine.

FIRST FIREMAN
(compassionately to Man)
Tough luck, partner!

MAN
(helplessly—to Blackie)
My house is burning.
Blackie looks at him—the man turns and walks AWAY. Blackie turns to the fireman.

BLACKIE
Is the Grenoble Hotel all right?
The fireman calls down to Blackie from the truck,

FIREMAN
Couldn't tell you, brother.
The fire truck starts to drive off. Blackie, having partly regained his breath, paying no attention—looking straight ahead—goes on down the street.

DISSOLVE TO:

GRENOBLE HOTEL STREET
The street in front of the Grenoble. The hotel is a small, exclusive hotel on top of a hill—partly wrecked by the earthquake. BLACKIE, exhausted, doggedly making his way down the street, ENTERS. The air is filled with smoke. In b.g. we see REFUGEES going by, dragging hastily rescued goods on every conceivable vehicle (carpet sweepers packed with goods, sewing machines piled high with articles, bed springs to the corners of which roller skates are attached.) One man is dragging a trunk over the pavement, which makes an unearthly SCREECHING NOISE. Blackie reaches the front of the hotel and sees TWO CHILDREN and their CHINESE NURSE (who holds a third child, a BABY, in her arms) sitting on some luggage, waiting.

BLACKIE
(to the group)
D'you live here?

The nurse stares glassy eyed, saying nothing.

> LITTLE GIRL

Yes.

> BLACKIE

Have you seen Miss Blake? She was in a white ball dress.

The children shake their heads. Blackie starts into the hotel, then choked by the smoke, starts to COUGH. He stops.

> BLACKIE
> (to Nurse)

Better get those kids to an open space!

The nurse still stares, glassy eyed.

> LITTLE GIRL

We're waiting for Mother and Daddy.

Blackie gestures toward the hotel.

> BLACKIE

Are they in there?

> LITTLE GIRL

No.

> (with simple faith)

But they'll come home.

Blackie turns, goes on into the hotel, passing a POLICEMAN who comes down the street steering a MAN who has gone insane.

INT   LOBBY OF HOTEL

BLACKIE ENTERS and looks about. The lobby is deserted. The chandelier lies in a heap on the floor, among large chunks of plaster.

> BLACKIE
> (calling out)

Is anybody here?

> BELLBOY (OS)

Who is it?

Blackie looks up. A BELLBOY APPEARS, coming down the stairway, carrying an OLD WOMAN who lies inert in his arms.

> BLACKIE

Is Mary Blake here?

> BELLBOY

She lived here—but she hasn't been back since the quake. We're getting everyone out—the fire's creeping up.

Blackie turns dazedly and goes OUT.

GRENOBLE HOTEL STREET   CHILDREN   NURSE
As BLACKIE comes out, the little girl waiting in front of the hotel—

> LITTLE GIRL
> (calls out)

Mother—Daddy!

SCREAMING WITH JOY the children, followed by the nurse, rush into the arms of a dishevelled COUPLE in evening dress who hurry down the street INTO THE SHOT. There are frantic EX-CLAMATIONS OF JOY as they embrace. The MOTHER sinks to her knees.

> LITTLE GIRL
> (repeats over and over)

We knew you'd come!

Blackie looks at the above scene dazedly, shaken by the emotion of it, becoming thoughtful that perhaps it was faith which brought these people together. He stands hesitant a moment, almost as if going to pray, then pulling himself up he shakes off the mood, turns and goes doggedly on. He goes to the top of the hill where he stops and looks off the hill over the city.

LONG SHOT   CITY   DAY
Fires are spotted all over the city.

> DISSOLVE TO:

LONG SHOT   CITY   NIGHT
Fires are burning in larger areas.

> DISSOLVE TO:

ANOTHER STREET   BLACKIE   NIGHT
The street is lit by the flickering glare of fire. Blackie is stumbling

along the street, dazed, exhausted, hardly able to keep on. O.s.
we hear a cart going over cobbles and debris and—

                    SALVATION ARMY MAN (OS)
     Want a lift, brother?
Blackie looks up. He sees the cart, driven by a SALVATION
ARMY MAN.

                    BLACKIE
     Where you going?

                    SALVATION ARMY MAN
     To San Marino—to get milk for kids.

                    BLACKIE
                    (declining)
     Thanks.
The man starts to drive on.

                    BLACKIE (cont'd)
                    (calling after)
     Say—if you see a red-haired girl in a white ball dress,
     tell her *Blackie's looking for her*, will you?

                    SALVATION ARMY MAN
                    (calling back)
     I'll be glad to. May God help you find her.
By which time the CART is OUT OF THE SHOT. Blackie stands in
the flickering glare of the distant fire, looking after the cart,
thinking, trying to bring himself to pray—but he cannot. He
finally gives up and stumbles on.
                                        DISSOLVE TO:

ANOTHER STREET   BLACKIE
Blackie moves along, further exhausted, but his attitude still one
of insistent intent. He passes a deserted house in front of which
a little DOG with a broken leg lies WHINING. Blackie stops—
looks at dog.

                    BLACKIE
     No use hanging around here, you poor little sucker.
He goes on. The dog gets up and limps after him. They go a little

ways when Blackie stops and looks down. The dog looks up at him in appeal.

> BLACKIE
> Look here, pal. I can't help you.

Blackie continues on—the dog does, too. Blackie looks back, hesitates—then stops, picks up the dog and goes on.

DISSOLVE TO:

CLOSE SHOT   TIM'S MISSION   BLACKIE   NEAR DAWN
Blackie, carrying the dog, comes down the street.

> SOLDIER (OS)
> Better get back from the wreckage, partner.

CAMERA PULLS BACK TO REVEAL front of Tim's Mission. The Mission is in ruins. A SOLDIER is stationed on guard.

> BLACKIE
> I'm looking for the priest that used to be here.

> SOLDIER
> Think he's doing rescue work at the stable next to the car barns.

> BLACKIE
> Thanks.

Almost despairing, he turns to go—then stops.

> BLACKIE (cont'd)
> Have you seen anything of a girl in a white—

> SOLDIER
> (kindly)
> Sorry—I just got here from the Presidio.

As he turns to go, TWO STRETCHER BEARERS ENTER THE SHOT, carrying a MAN ON STRETCHER with broken leg.

> BLACKIE
> (to First Stretcher Bearer)
> Hold on there, pal. Here's another fellow with a broken leg.

Blackie puts the dog on the stretcher and goes on.

A Screenplay 177

MAN ON STRETCHER
(to dog)
You got three legs and I've only got one. What are you
kicking about?

DISSOLVE TO:

FRONT OF STABLE   BLACKIE
Blackie staggers down the street. As he nears the stable, TWO
SOLDIERS come down the street carrying a stretcher on which is
an INJURED MAN.

INJURED MAN
(screaming out—delirious)
Fire! Fire! The fire's coming! Get me out!
THEY ENTER the stable, followed by Blackie.

INT   STABLE
BLACKIE ENTERS, stands a moment looking dazedly off. The
stable is feebly lit by church candles in church candlesticks. In
b.g. the injured, dying and dead are lying in the stalls. Working
about among them is TIM—his clothes blackened, torn and half
stripped off. He is lifting an injured man from a stretcher and
placing him on a cot. An older priest, called MONSIGNOR, is
in charge, and there are several PRIESTS, one administering to a
DYING GIRL who, half delirious, keeps intoning throughout the
scene:

DYING GIRL
Oh my God, I am sorry for having offended Thee/And I
detest all my sins./Because I have offended Thee, My
God/Who art all good and deserving of all my love,/I
resolve with the help of Thy grace/To confess my sins/
To do penance/And to amend my life/Amen.
Several women, one of them a Salvation Army Girl, are helping
out in the nursing. Among the victims are two Chinamen and a
Negro. Blackie sees Tim and heads for him. He goes past a cot
on which lies MAT. Beside him stands a Salvation Army Girl
with a glass of water from which she has been giving him a
drink.

> MAT
> (calls feebly)

Hello, Blackie.

Blackie stops—sees him—then dazedly—beginning further to soften and break down:

> BLACKIE

Hello.

Mat swells with pride.

> MAT
>
> Those cops couldn't hang onto me. I got away from them.

> BLACKIE

Did you? That's great!

> MAT
>
> Sure! It took the *earthquake* to get me!

> BLACKIE
> (touched)
>
> How you making, kid?

> MAT
> (obviously lying)

Aw—I'll pull through.

> BLACKIE
> (overly emphatic)

Sure you will!

He glances up at the Salvation Army Girl. She looks back at Blackie, her expression telling him that Mat is dying. Changing the subject,

> MAT
>
> I heard Mary went on for you at the Chickens' Ball. I was wrong about her, Blackie.
> (smiles)

She's a great kid.

Blackie looks at him, tears welling into his eyes. He cannot speak, but he pats Mat's shoulder in response, then turning to the Salvation Army Girl:

BLACKIE

Don't leave him.

SALVATION ARMY GIRL

I won't.

Blackie goes on toward Tim, approaching him and:

BLACKIE
(almost with supplication)

Tim!

Tim looks up—sees him. It is the first time they have seen each
other since the night Blackie knocked Tim down. There is a long,
long PAUSE as they look at each other. A great rush of feeling
wells up between them which they cannot put into words. Finally:

BLACKIE

I can't find Mary, Tim!

Tim studies him a moment, beginning to sense his chastened
being.

BLACKIE (cont'd)

You got to help me find her!

TIM

What do you want to find her for, Blackie? The Paradise
is gone.

BLACKIE

I don't want her for the Paradise.

He turns and starts out. Tim's elated—his face lighting up.

TIM

Wait a minute!

Blackie stops. Tim calls off to a NUN who is passing.

TIM (cont'd)

Sister Agatha.

She stops. Tim gestures to the man on the cot.

TIM (cont'd)

Look after him, will you?

                              NUN
          Yes, Father.
Tim turns, joins Blackie who stands watching dazedly. He leads
Blackie toward the Monsignor who is bandaging a Chinaman's
broken arm.

                              TIM
          Monsignor—I'd like to leave a while . . . to help a
          friend.

                          MONSIGNOR
          Go ahead, my son.

                              TIM
          Come on, Blackie.
Tim and Blackie go on, Tim taking his coat from a nail by the
door and putting it on as they go. O.s. we hear the first sound of
DISTANT DYNAMITING.

EXT   STABLE   DAWN
TIM and BLACKIE COME OUT. Dawn is just breaking, but the
light, filtering through the smoke, is cold, flat and cheerless.
O.s. another sound of DYNAMITING. They both look off.

STREET   BUILDING   BLACKIE'S POV
In the far distance we see a big building being DYNAMITED. It
CRASHES.

STREET   BLACKIE   TIM
Tim and Blackie look off aghast at the spectacle of the dynamited
building. Some MARINES go by in a truck. To a MARINE in the
street,

                              TIM
          What are the explosions?

                           MARINE
          They're dynamiting to stop the fire.
Tim turns to Blackie,

                              TIM
          Have you looked for her around Lyric Hall?

BLACKIE
(dazedly)
I looked as well as I could . . . alone. I found Burley.
The quake got him. They were together.

TIM
(sickened)
The soldiers are working there now. We'll try again.
A PAUSE—he stands a moment in silent prayer, Blackie watching him fixedly—dazedly. Finally Tim snaps out of his prayer—
turns to Blackie:

TIM
(matter-of-factly)
Come on, kid!
They go OFF. O.s. the BOOM of dynamiting.

DISSOLVE TO:

EXT   LYRIC HALL   TIM   BLACKIE
It is a mass of broken masonry and timbers. Tim and Blackie are
looking among the debris. In b.g. we see SOLDIERS also removing debris, looking for bodies. The fire is creeping up. O.s. in-
cessant BOOM of dynamiting—now much LOUDER. Two soldiers go by with an army stretcher on which is a body covered
by a sheet. They stop.

FIRST SOLDIER
(kindly)
Are you fellows looking for a red-haired girl?
Tim and Blackie stop—look at each other. Blackie takes a step
toward the stretcher. Stopping Blackie,

TIM
Wait!
He goes to the stretcher, lifts the sheet, under which we see the
girl's mass of red hair. Blackie, watching, doesn't breathe. Tim
brushes back the girl's hair.

BLACKIE
(bursting out)
Is it—

                          TIM
        No.
Tim quickly crosses himself. Then to one of the soldiers.

                     TIM (cont'd)
            She's not the one.

                    SECOND SOLDIER
                      (to Blackie)
          Hope you find her okay, pal!
They carry the body OFF. O.s. a LOUDER BOOM of dynamiting.
Blackie and Tim look off.

BUILDING   BLACKIE'S POV
The building CRUMBLES under the dynamiting.

EXT   LYRIC HALL   TIM   BLACKIE
They turn from the dynamited building.

                       BLACKIE
                      (sickened)
             They're getting nearer.
Tim looks down at an enormous beam.

                         TIM
            Give me a hand, Blackie.
Blackie helps Tim to lift the beam. O.s. DYNAMITING very close.
We glimpse a man's body crumpled under the beam. As they
stand looking at the body, a MARINE with dynamiting apparatus
comes over.

                        MARINE
        We've got to dynamite, boys. You'll have to leave.
Tim gently lowers the beam back onto the body and turns to
Blackie.

                         TIM
        All we can do is keep trying. Come on, Blackie.
They start off making their way over the debris. Presently we
hear:

                     MARINE (OS)
            Look out, everybody!

Tim and Blackie look back.

LYRIC HALL   BLACKIE'S POV
The hall is DYNAMITED.

TIM   BLACKIE
Tim and Blackie walk on—enveloped in a cloud of smoke and dust from the dynamiting. For a long moment they say nothing. Finally—

                          BLACKIE
          I don't know why you want to help me, Tim.
Tim looks at him—smiles.

                          TIM
          Don't you?
They walk along further in SILENCE. O.s. we hear the DYNA-MITING. Finally:

                          BLACKIE
          I thought you and I had gotten awfully far apart.

                          TIM
          I didn't.
Blackie takes hold of his arm. He squeezes it. They continue in SILENCE.

                                        DISSOLVE TO:

VALENCIA HOTEL STREET   DAY
The o.s. DYNAMITING CONTINUES. In b.g. we see fire raging. The four-story hotel has sunk until the top floor is level with the street. A POLICEMAN stands on guard to keep people away. In b.g. a few straggling REFUGEES are going down the street, dragging possessions with them. There are several heavy trunks being dragged along making an UNCANNY SCREECHING SOUND. BLACKIE AND TIM come down the street—stop and look at the hotel.

                          TIM
                  (to policeman, aghast)
          That was four stories high, wasn't it?

POLICEMAN

Yep.

TIM

Did they save many?

POLICEMAN

Those on the top floor stepped right out their windows to the street. The others were out of luck.

Tim and Blackie stand looking at the hotel, dazed, horrified, when HAZELTINE (the heckler of the Rally episode) hurries down the street. Never stopping,

HAZELTINE
(joyfully)

Hello, Blackie! I just got word of my kid! He's safe in Oakland!

BLACKIE
(from his heart)

That's fine.

Tim turns to Blackie.

TIM

We haven't tried Nob Hill—the Burley home.

BLACKIE
(tonelessly)

No.

TIM

There's one other place . . . her teacher's, Mme. Albani's.
(a moment's thought, then—)
You go to Nob Hill—I'll try Albani's. I'll meet you at the corner of Octavia and Fillmore Streets.

Without a word Blackie turns and heads for Nob Hill. Tim looks after him a moment—then goes in the other direction. At which point from the ruins of the Valencia a DRUNK steps out the front window in his night shirt and silk hat, a bottle in his hand. Looking about at the destruction,

DRUNK

What happened?

DISSOLVE TO:

NOB HILL   BLACKIE   DAY
Blackie starts up Nob Hill, with burning city in b.g. The heat is intense—his hair is matted with dirt, blood and perspiration, and he is nearing exhaustion. The smoke is dense. He stops in the middle of the street and looks off.

BURLEY MANSION   FIREMEN   MARINES   BLACKIE'S POV
The Burley house—Firemen and Marines are seen moving about through the smoke. Out of the house comes MRS. MAIZIE BURLEY, followed by several servants, all of whom are loaded with hastily gathered up articles.

NOB HILL   BLACKIE
Seeing Mrs. Burley o.s., Blackie calls off:

BLACKIE

Mrs. Burley . . .

He exits in her direction.

BURLEY MANSION   MRS. BURLEY   SERVANTS   BUTLER
Mrs. Burley and her retinue, including a seedy-looking butler, come away from the mansion. BLACKIE ENTERS THE SCENE, crosses the street toward the sidewalk. Mrs. Burley turns and they face each other.

BLACKIE

Mrs. Burley, have you seen Mary Blake?

MRS. BURLEY

She was with my son.
(then quickly)
He's a fine boy, my Jack—fine and strong, like his father. He never means any harm, his heart is full of goodness. He's a fine son . . . He's dead, isn't he?

Blackie cannot meet her gaze. It is her confirmation. Trying to accept her fate,

MRS. BURLEY (cont'd)
It's—God's will . . .

But she falters under the blow, and impulsively Blackie puts his
arms clear around her. She leans against him and weeps on his
bosom. (To Maizie this is almost as if the man she loved in her
youth, who was so like Blackie, has returned and is comforting
her.) There is a PAUSE. As he holds her in his arms, we have the
tenderness of a man who, for many years, has had no mother of
his own. After the mood is thoroughly established, a MARINE
ENTERS THE SCENE. With kindly brusqueness—hating to be
officious:

MARINE
You'll have to move on, Mrs. Burley. We're dynamiting.

BLACKIE
(resentfully)
Can't you wait a minute?

Feeling the tenseness of the situation,

MARINE
(kindly—from the heart)
Sorry, but—

Mrs. Burley's head comes up from Blackie's chest; she does not
look at him.

MRS. BURLEY
It doesn't matter.

She starts to move on. Blackie helps her, with his arm around
her. They EXIT THE SCENE.

NOB HILL STREET
BLACKIE AND MRS. BURLEY ENTER. They are moving very
slowly. The burning city is seen in b.g. below. We hear the
SHOUTS of the Marines in back of them. Blackie looks back over
his shoulder.

BURLEY MANSION   BLACKIE'S POV
The EXPLOSION! The house breaks, rises and settles in ruins.

NOB HILL STREET   BLACKIE   MRS. BURLEY
Blackie looks at the house o.s. Mrs. Burley stops, turns and looks back.

> MRS. BURLEY
> My boy was born there.

BURLEY MANSION   MRS. BURLEY'S POV
And now the debris is BLOWN UP.

NOB HILL STREET   BLACKIE   MRS. BURLEY
Mrs. Burley turns, starts OUT OF SCENE away from Blackie's protecting arms. Blackie hurries after her.

> BLACKIE
> Let me help you, Mrs. Burley.

BURLEY MANSION   MRS. BURLEY   BLACKIE
Mrs. Burley looks up at Blackie. In b.g. is Burley home debris. Mrs. Burley is strong in her faith, almost smiling, as:

> MRS. BURLEY
> Thanks, Blackie Norton. It's God's help we both need now. Good-bye.

Resolutely she walks OUT OF SCENE, leaving Blackie looking after her, reacting to her mention of God. He stands a moment—deeply thoughtful. He finally shifts his position to look out over the burning city, where he sees DYNAMITING o.s. He reacts to the dynamiting.

LONG SHOT   CITY   DAY
The burning city, with more DYNAMITING going on.
> DISSOLVE TO:

LONG SHOT   CITY   NIGHT
The city is still ablaze—DYNAMITING goes on incessantly.
> DISSOLVE TO:

STREET CORNER   NEAR MORNING
It is very nearly morning. We see a breadline which has been organized in a vacant lot. People are waiting for their rations. BLACKIE comes in wearily to the breadline, starts moving along,

looking at the people there. Various types, lower class to upper class, are in line. Suddenly he hears:

> MAN (OS)
> (hysterical with joy)
> Mary, Mary!

The MAN goes past Blackie. Blackie follows the man eagerly. A GIRL, not resembling Mary Blake at all, comes forward to meet the man, and throws her arms about him. Weeping with joy as she embraces the man,

> GIRL
> Oh, thank God! Thank God my prayers have been answered!

The man is weeping in happiness, too—holding her close.

> MAN
> Mary, Mary, my darling!

Blackie looks at their joy, then stumbles on down the breadline, dazed, frantic, looking ahead through the motley lineup of people as he goes. A MAN IN BREADLINE, seeing Blackie's exhaustion, moves back to make place for Blackie ahead of him.

> MAN IN BREADLINE
> Come on in here, partner.

Blackie stops, touched to the heart by the man's kindness.

> BLACKIE
> (kindly, but in negation)
> Thanks, pal.

He starts dazedly on, stops, leans against a lamppost. Then, he comes ahead very wearily and sees the FORRESTALLS. FORRESTALL is bandaged, one leg in splints—home-made crutch. They're drinking soup. Blackie stops and looks at them.

> FORRESTALL
> Hello, Norton.

> BLACKIE
> Hello. Say, did you see Mary Blake—you know—the girl who sang—

                     MRS. FORRESTALL
No, we haven't.

                     BLACKIE
Thanks.
Indicating Forrestall's condition,

                     BLACKIE (cont'd)
Sorry you're—

                     FORRESTALL
Oh, I'm all right.
Forrestall LAUGHS slightly.

                     FORRESTALL (cont'd)
All we have left is a plate of soup, but we're alive, thank God—both of us.
He looks at his wife adoringly. She takes his hand.

                     BLACKIE
Well, so long.
Blackie starts away.

                     FORRESTALL
         (calls after him)
Oh, Norton—
Blackie turns.

                     FORRESTALL (cont'd)
Anything we can do for you, let me know.

                     BLACKIE
Thanks.
He goes on. Leaving the FORRESTALLS behind, Blackie looks around, leans weakly against something. A TOUGH-LOOKING MAN comes up to him.

                     TOUGH-LOOKING MAN
What's the matter, buddy—hungry? Let me get you some beans.

                     BLACKIE
No—no, thanks. Say, you didn't see a red—
Blackie stops—realizing it's useless.

TOUGH-LOOKING MAN
Lose somebody?

BLACKIE
Yeah—I'm afraid so.

TOUGH-LOOKING MAN
That's tough. My old lady got out all right—the kid, too. I don't know how I rated it, but God was certainly good to me. I'm goin' to do things different after this. Sure I can't get you some beans?

BLACKIE
No, thanks.

MAN IN CROWD (OS)
(calls out)
Oh, Jim.

TOUGH-LOOKING MAN
(to Blackie)
Well, so long.
The TOUGH-LOOKING MAN EXITS. Blackie looks after him a second, then goes over and sits down.

ANOTHER STREET   BLACKIE   EARLY MORNING
We pick up Blackie walking along in the fog—early morning—as he's coming toward the corner of Octavia and Sacramento Streets. As he nears the corner, we see TIM standing in the wet fog, waiting—his coat collar pulled up. Blackie looks at him.

TIM
I've found her!
Blackie PAUSES—then:

BLACKIE
Is she—all right?

TIM
Yes, she's all right. Come on.
He takes Blackie by the arm and leads him OFF.
DISSOLVE TO:

LAFAYETTE SQUARE   BLACKIE   TIM

Tim and Blackie are going up the hill toward Lafayette Square, passing REFUGEES, who, loaded with provisions, goods, etc., are headed in the same direction. Blackie and Tim go on in SILENCE. Then:

BLACKIE

Does she know I'm—
(he breaks off)

TIM

She knows you're safe.

Presently o.s. we begin to hear the strains of "Nearer My God to Thee" being SUNG by a number of people—interspersed with infrequent distant DYNAMITING. As they approach the entrance to the Square, one voice rises among all the others—it is MARY'S. Blackie listens and his face lights up with joy. They hurry on, reaching a high vantage point in the Square where they stop and look. A number of refugees are gathered about MARY who, her white dress hanging in rags, her hair falling about her shoulders, sits SINGING, a little dead child in her arms—the child's mother kneels at her feet, softly SOBBING. Blackie stands transfixed, looking at Mary. Tears of emotion welling up into his eyes,

BLACKIE

I want to thank God, Tim. What do I say?

TIM

Say what's in your heart, Blackie.

Blackie sinks to his knees—Tim watching him, tears welling into his eyes.

BLACKIE

Thanks, God! Thanks . . . I really mean it.

A Protestant minister, in gray suit and solid white collar, is ministering to the child as Mary and the group continue SINGING. The minister picks up the dead child and carries it into a tent. Mary looks up and sees Blackie praying. Blackie's head drops in silent prayer. Then, Mary gets up and goes toward

Blackie, the others continuing to SING. As she approaches him, Blackie sees her coming. He gets to his feet, takes a step toward her, then hesitates. Mary continues and goes to him. They look at each other, too much in their hearts to speak. Suddenly:

> SOMEONE (OS)
> (hollering)
> The fire is out! The fire is out!

They react to this, and Blackie puts his arm around Mary as they walk together. Mary takes up the SONG as they walk. Blackie looks into Mary's eyes. And Mary looks up at Blackie. Mary, Blackie and Tim climb the hill, Mary SINGING. They are surrounded by people, some SINGING; all have ecstatic expressions of joy on their faces.

TOP OF HILL   BLACKIE   MARY   TIM   OTHERS
We see the faces of the crowd as they look over the burning city, SINGING THE FINALE. The foreground of the slope of the hill toward the city is packed with people, as is the background, as far as we can see. Mary, Blackie and Tim stand in relief with those on the crest of the hill.

CLOSE SHOT   MARY   BLACKIE   TIM
As they look over the city, Mary SINGING ecstatically. Mary and Blackie look at each other and . . .

FADE OUT.

THE END

Afterword

By Anita Loos

It is revealing to look back on work written years ago; generally it discloses why some material stands the test of time better than others. And it becomes obvious that any story that's rooted in strong *personal* feelings outlasts a contrived plot, no matter how clever.

The idea of writing *San Francisco* came to Robert Hopkins, my collaborator, and me out of our mutual love for the exciting city where we had spent our childhood. The two of us never met in San Francisco, but early in the thirties I went to Hollywood to join the writing staff at MGM and there formed a lasting friendship with Bob Hopkins (or Hoppy as everyone at the studio called him). Hoppy's position in the scenario department was unique. It had nothing to do with writing. He had been hired by our studio boss, Irving Thalberg, to inject jokes, ad lib, into any scripts that tended to be dull. Hoppy was the studio's one and only "gag man."

Now Hoppy and I happened to share a particular distaste for Southern California, one which is the heritage of all natives of San Francisco. We delighted in memories of the city of our youth; its brisk Northern climate generates energy, just as the tepid air of Southern California dissipates it. We had a deep love for ancient San Francisco landmarks, of which the entire Los Angeles area had none; we cherished the free-and-easy spirit of forebears who had risked their lives crossing the plains in covered wagons, suffered tremendous hardships, and fallen afoul of attacks by Indians to reach their Eldorado. We shared an equal contempt for those citizens of Southern California who had none of the imagination and braggadocio that motivated our own colorful pioneers.

One day when the two of us were pacing the broad main alley

of the MGM studio, voicing our nostalgia for San Francisco, it crossed our minds to make its romantic charm the subject of a movie. It wasn't necessary to search for a character who might symbolize the spirit of our city. We had both known him for years. His name was Wilson Mizner, and he had begun his adventurous career as a gambler on the Barbary Coast of San Francisco.

Now Hoppy, as a boy, had been a Western Union messenger on the Barbary Coast. He had run errands for the clientele of a glamorous gambling casino where Wilson hung out and where the handsome young adventurer had become Hoppy's idol. I had met Wilson at a later period in various capitals of the world, where his life was as full of adventure as it had ever been in San Francisco. Wilson and I became close friends. And it later came about that Wilson was drawn to Hollywood as the world's newest frontier for adventure. Thus Hoppy and I were able to enjoy our friend's matchless companionship and wit for the last few years of his life.

Inspired by memories of Wilson, Hoppy and I began to improvise a story—partly out of love for our now departed pal; partly out of nostalgia for our home town—and, during the process, to contrast San Francisco's romantic spirit with the grubbiness of Southern California.

We finally took our idea to Irving Thalberg. Now Hoppy, as a gag man, had never worked on a full length story, but Irving was impressed. Furthermore, he himself had known and secretly appreciated Wilson Mizner. "Go ahead," said he. "Put something down on paper. We'll see if it's worth filming." Our collaboration proceeded, with Hoppy talking out his ideas while I did the paper work. And from time to time we went to Irving to report progress. Steadily his interest mounted. "It's beginning to look like a natural for Clark Gable," said Irving.

For years Irving had been warned by doctors to slow his pace, but he felt it better to die of overwork than be bored to death by inactivity. Just as Hoppy and I were finishing our script, Irving's frail health failed, and he turned the production over to his greatest disciple among the staff of MGM producers, Bernard Hyman. But poor Bernie had been raised in the Bronx, and it became clear during our early conferences that Bernie could never understand our hero, who was as fastidious as he was ruthless. Hoppy and I finished our final script of *San Francisco*, and it was okayed by Bernie on 15 January 1936. The movie opened in New York on 27 June 1936, only two months before Irving Thalberg died. His death, while still in his thirties, plunged us into deep despair.

San Francisco became the most important issue in the lives of both Hoppy and me. To him it meant a graduation from "gag man" to "author." And, most of all, our film would be the means of waving a last goodbye to Wilson Mizner.

MGM was trying to build up the career of an unknown contract player, and the front office ordered Bernie to put that colorless neophyte into a part that could be played only by Gable. Difficulties kept on mounting; the next setback turned out to be a serious brush with the board of censors. It protested a sequence in which our antihero, bent on exploiting an innocent girl in a notorious dive on the Barbary Coast, met with the violent opposition of a young Catholic priest. And in a rousing battle between those forces of Good and Evil, our antihero hauled off and knocked the good priest out cold.

The administrator for the censor board, Joe Breen, sent for Hoppy and me and said grimly, "Look here, folks, we can't allow that so-called hero of yours to humiliate a Catholic priest." We argued that our story told of the regeneration of an evil man. Unless he were violently wicked, his regeneration wouldn't be very dramatic. But it appeared that a censor's idea of regeneration was to establish that a character is rather naughty and then allow him to improve.

"Your hero's regeneration takes place toward the end of the script," protested Breen. "In the meantime a priest has been degraded in a way that will bring the entire Catholic Church down on us." Hoppy and I felt that the Catholic Church had an understanding of artistic values, but Breen wouldn't agree. We had to delete the sequence.

The next day we were cursing the idiotic shortsightedness of censors who were emasculating our story when Hoppy suddenly thought of asking for help from the priest of the small Catholic chapel across the boulevard from the studio. Father Benedict was very movie-wise. He was often sent for to advise on religious scenes; his confessional was frequently visited by show-biz sinners; all of which made him tremendously understanding and sympathetic to movies. Father Ben heard our problem out and racked his brains. Then presently his face lit up. "I've thought of something that may save your precious scene," said he.

Following Father Ben's suggestion, we went to work and invented the scene he suggested. The next day we took it to Joe Breen, and Hoppy proceeded to defend our sequence as if he were Shakespeare fighting to keep the soliloquy from being tossed out of *Hamlet*.

The episode we had devised took place in a gymnasium where we showed a friendly boxing match between our anti-hero and our priest, in the course of which we established that the husky young priest could easily outbox, outslug, and outsmart our antihero. Then, when the two men faced their moment of truth, the priest would *purposely* allow himself to be knocked out; thus "presenting the other cheek" and making our priest the hero of the encounter. I knew our solution was weak but Hoppy's fast-talk finally won out over the censors. *San Francisco* was granted the go-ahead.

Now Bernie had managed to secure the great Woody Van Dyke to direct our film. This was a triumph, for Woody was the hero of MGM's latest smash hit, *White Shadows in the South Seas*. And having snared that ace director gave Bernie the crunch to demand Gable. We got him, with Clark's full cooperation . . . he too had known Wilson Mizner. But no sooner did the filming start than Hoppy and I realized we faced a new disaster. Van Dyke, who was capable of understanding the mentality of South Sea savages, was an oaf when it came to the subtleties of the San Francisco Tenderloin.

We were horrified watching a scene in the projection room where our hero reproved an underworld sweetheart for wearing a gaudy necklace. All of Clark Gable's native charm could never have overcome the loutish behavior in which he'd been directed by Van Dyke. We hurried to Bernie's office to demand a retake.

Bernie was surprised. "Why, I thought the way Woody directed that scene was swell!" For over an hour Hoppy and I invoked the principle of Irving Thalberg that one crass move on the part of any character in any film can cause it to flounder beyond recall. Bernie, bless his simple heart, finally got our viewpoint. He ordered the sequence reshot with Hoppy on the set in the future to guide Van Dyke. And from that point on, things went relatively well.

San Francisco has become a permanent survivor on the late, late TV programs, and I believe it is due to the fact that its authors had such deep feelings for their subject. We were homesick for San Francisco; we adored our pal who epitomized its lusty spirit, and thus were our sentiments strong enough to keep that movie alive and well in television through all these years.

Only recently the *New York Times* scheduled our film in its weekly TV section:

Thursday, 1:30 A.M. "San Francisco" (made in 1936) Clark Gable, Jeanette MacDonald, Spencer Tracy.
The works: love, opera and that super-duper earthquake. Grand show.

Postscript

It might be interesting to here paraphrase some key scenes of our script to explain how Hoppy and I established our major themes. The following episode occurs early in the movie and shows our feelings about the difference between the natives of San Francisco and Los Angeles:

A drunken lout is seated in the Paradise saloon with one of its girl "entertainers."

> DRUNK
> (calling off to singer on stage)
> Your singing stinks!

> GIRL
> Sh! You mustn't hurt the artist's feelings.

In protest the Drunk throws a handful of confetti into the girl's glass of beer. By this time a waiter enters scene to relieve the girl of annoyance.

> WAITER
> (to Drunk, quite genially)
> Come on out, pal.

He starts to steer the Drunk toward the door.

> DRUNK
> (again calling to singer)
> Aw shut up!

> WAITER
> (suddenly getting an idea, stops)
> . . . Say!—Where are you from?

> DRUNK
> (proudly)

Los Angeles!

BABE

I thought so!

Saying which, he looks around to be sure he's unobserved. Then, still holding the Drunk with one hand, gives him a short, quick sock on the button and knocks him cold.

The following scene is the one which saved our film from being destroyed by the board of censors:

FADE IN ON: A GYMNASIUM.

In background can be seen street types exercising, swinging clubs, etc., etc. Close shot of Gable in role of Blackie Norton. He is boxing with a husky young man, Tim Mullin, played by Spencer Tracy. One of Blackie's minions, Mat, comes up to watch them box a moment—then—

MAT

Blackie, I came over to tell you that the girl singer you hired last night didn't show up.

BLACKIE

(none too interested)

. . . That so? Well, forget her.

TIM

She wasn't any good, eh?

BLACKIE

. . . *Good?*

(chuckling sarcastically)

Why, her father is a preacher!

MAT

Gee—that's an old gag!

TIM

Well—maybe her father *is* a preacher!

BLACKIE

(to Mat)

Tim still believes in Santy Claus!

>TIM
>The trouble with Blackie is he doesn't believe in anything!

>BLACKIE
>That's where I'm smart!

He lands a pretty good sock on Tim.

>TIM
>Did you say *smart*?

>BLACKIE
>*That's what I said!*

At which Tim lands a sharp quick sock that flattens Blackie to the floor.

>MAT
>Gee! That guy sure packs a wallop!

>BLACKIE
>(trying to get his breath)
>Yeah. For twenty years the big mug has mauled me around and made a chump out of me and I always come back for more!

The following scene shows our priest turning the other cheek:

Mary, wearing the scanty garb of a cafe entertainer, is in Blackie's arms. They kiss, after which she speaks diffidently.

>MARY
>Blackie—let's set the date for our wedding, so we can tell Father Tim, eh?

>BLACKIE
>(evasively)
>Well, sure—the first chance I get I'll let you slip that halter on me.

Kisses her lightly on the forehead.

202 Postscript

BLACKIE (cont'd)
Never thought I'd be so nuts about *anyone!*
O.s. a knock on door.

BLACKIE (cont'd)
Come in.
TIM enters and reacts in shock at Mary's seminudity.

BLACKIE
(glibly)
Hello, Tim.

MARY
(abashed, tries to cover her deep décolletage)
Good evening, Father.

BLACKIE
What's wrong?

TIM
Are you getting ready to show Mary—like this—to that
mob out there!

BLACKIE
Look, Tim! I'm going to make Mary the Queen of the
Coast! See that poster! Five thousand of 'em will be
plastered all over Frisco tomorrow! And ten thousand
little ones—for ash cans and the front of trolley cars.

TIM
I'm not going to let you do this, Blackie.

BLACKIE
Come here, Mary!
Mary joins Blackie. He puts his arm about her.

BLACKIE (cont'd)
Will you tell his "holiness" you made up your own
mind to sing in my joint?

MARY
. . . I love him, Father.